S. Hrg. 115–166

CIVILIAN CONTROL OF THE ARMED FORCES

HEARING

BEFORE THE

COMMITTEE ON ARMED SERVICES
UNITED STATES SENATE

ONE HUNDRED FIFTEENTH CONGRESS

FIRST SESSION

JANUARY 10, 2017

Printed for the use of the Committee on Armed Services

Available via the World Wide Web: http://www.fdsys.gov/

U.S. GOVERNMENT PUBLISHING OFFICE

28–836 PDF   WASHINGTON : 2018

For sale by the Superintendent of Documents, U.S. Government Publishing Office
Internet: bookstore.gpo.gov   Phone: toll free (866) 512–1800; DC area (202) 512–1800
Fax: (202) 512–2104   Mail: Stop IDCC, Washington, DC 20402–0001

CONTENTS

CIVILIAN CONTROL OF THE ARMED FORCES

TUESDAY, JANUARY 10, 2017

U.S. SENATE,
COMMITTEE ON ARMED SERVICES,
Washington, DC.

The committee met, pursuant to notice, at 9:29 a.m. in Room SH–216, Hart Senate Office Building, Senator John McCain (chairman) presiding.

Committee members present: Senators McCain, Inhofe, Wicker, Fischer, Cotton, Rounds, Ernst, Sullivan, Perdue, Reed, Nelson, Shaheen, Gillibrand, Blumenthal, Donnelly, Hirono, Kaine, King, Heinrich, Warren, and Peters.

OPENING STATEMENT OF SENATOR JOHN McCAIN, CHAIRMAN

Chairman MCCAIN. The committee meets this morning to receive testimony on civilian control of the Armed Forces.

I'd like to welcome our witnesses: Dr. Eliot Cohen, Robert E. Osgood Professor of Strategic Studies at the Johns Hopkins School of Advanced International Studies—that's very impressive; Dr. Kathleen Hicks, also impressive, Senior Vice President, Kissinger Chair and Director of the International Security Program at the Center for Strategic and International Studies. Welcome.

Civilian control of the Armed Forces has been a bedrock principle of American government since our Revolution. A painting hanging in the Capitol Rotunda celebrates the legacy of George Washington, who voluntarily resigned his commission as Commander of the Continental Army to the Congress. This principle is enshrined in our Constitution, which divides control of the Armed Forces among the President, as Commander in Chief, and the Congress as co-equal branches of government. Since then, Congress has adopted various provisions separating military and civilian positions.

In the 19th century, for example, Congress prohibited an Army officer from accepting a civil office. More recently, in the National Security Act of 1947 and subsequent revisions, Congress has prohibited any individual from serving as Secretary of Defense within seven years of Active Duty service as a commissioned officer in the Armed Forces. Of course, it was only three years later, in 1950, that Congress granted General George Marshall an exemption to that law and the Senate confirmed him to be Secretary of Defense.

Indeed, the separation between civilian and military positions has not always been so clear. Twelve of our Nation's Presidents previously served as generals in the Armed Forces. Over the years, numerous high-ranking civilian officials in the Department of Defense have had long careers in military service. Our current Deputy

Secretary of Defense, for example, served 27 years in the United States Marine Corps.

The basic responsibilities of civilian and military leaders are simple enough: for civilian leaders, to seek the best professional military advice while under no obligation to follow it; for military leaders, to provide candid counsel while recognizing civilians have the final say or, as James Mattis once observed, to insist on being heard and never insist on being obeyed.

But, the fact is that the relationship between civilian and military leaders is inherently and endlessly complex. It is a relationship of unequals who nonetheless share responsibility for the defense of the Nation. The stakes could not be higher. The gaps in mutual understandings are sometimes wide, personalities often clash, and the unique features of the profession of arms and the peculiarities of service cultures often prove daunting for civilians who never served in uniform.

Ultimately, the key to healthy civil-military relations and civilian control of the military is the oath soldiers and statesmen share in common, to protect and defend the Constitution. It is about the trust they have in one another to perform their respective duties in accordance with our republican system of government. It is about the candid exchange of views engendered by that trust and which is vital to effective decisionmaking. It is about mutual respect and understanding.

The proper balance in civil-military relations is difficult to achieve, and, as history has taught us, achieving that balance requires different leaders at different times. The President-elect has announced his intention to nominate James Mattis to be our next Secretary of Defense. In light of his recent military experience, his nomination will require Congress to pass legislation providing a one-time exception allowing him to serve as Secretary, legislation this committee plans to consider this Thursday. The members of this committee will have to reach their own conclusion, but, as for me, I will fully support that legislation and Mr. Mattis's—and General Mattis's nomination. There is no military officer I have met in my lifetime with a deeper understanding of civil-military relations than James Mattis. He even co-edited a book on the subject. He has upheld the principle of civilian controlling the Armed Forces in four decades of military service, as well as in civilian life. His character, judgment, and commitment to defending our Nation and its Constitution have earned him the trust of our next Commander in Chief, Members of Congress on both sides of the aisle, and so many serving in our Armed Forces. In short, I believe James Mattis is an exceptional public servant worthy of exceptional consideration.

The committee is fortunate to have with us two of the foremost scholars on civil-military relations, both of whom have a record of distinguished government service. I'm eager to hear their views on this important subject. I'd like to add, it was the Ranking Member, Senator Reed's request and legitimate concern about this issue that we are having this hearing. I want to thank my friend, the Ranking Member, for making sure that this hearing is held.

Senator Reed.

3

Senator REED. Well, thank you very much, Mr. Chairman, for holding this hearing, because I do think, as you have indicated so well, how critical this issue is to the country.

Also let me welcome our distinguished witnesses, Dr. Eliot Cohen and Dr. Kathleen Hicks. Thank you very much for your scholarship and your service to the Nation.

Civilian control of the military is enshrined in our Constitution and dates back to General George Washington and the Revolutionary War. For almost 230 years, this principle has distinguished our Nation from many other countries around the world, and it has helped ensure that our democracy remains in the hands of the people.

When the Department of Defense was created by the National Security Act of 1947, the law included a stipulation that an individual appointed to serve as the Secretary of this new agency could not be within ten years of Active Duty as a commissioned officer in a regular component of the Armed Services. However, an exception to this statute was enacted into law shortly thereafter, in 1950, to permit George Marshall to serve as Secretary of Defense shortly after he concluded his service as Secretary of State. It then stood untouched for nearly six decades, until the Fiscal Year 2008 National Defense Authorization Act modified the requirement by reducing the integral from ten years to seven years. But, the principle was very clear, and still was sustained.

This requirement has served our Nation well for the past 70 years, and only once has Congress waived or modified this statute. For only the second time since the creation of the Department of Defense, Congress must make a determination if an exception should be made to allow recently retired General James Mattis to serve as the Secretary of Defense. As this committee considers legislation to provide an exception to General Mattis, I believe that it is extremely important that we carefully consider the consequences of setting aside the law and the implications such a decision may have on the future of civilian and military relations. We must always be very cautious about any actions that may inadvertently politicize our Armed Forces.

During this past presidential election cycle, both Democrats and Republicans came dangerously close to compromising the nonpartisan nature of our military when the nominating conventions featured speeches from recently retired general officers advocating for a candidate for President. As former Chairman of the Joint Chiefs of Staff, General Martin Dempsey, stated shortly after the conventions, "If senior military leaders, active and retired, begin to self-identify as members or supporters of one party or another, then the inherent tension built into our system of government between the executive branch and the legislative branch will bleed over into suspicion of military leaders by Congress and a further erosion of civilian-military relations." I hope our witnesses today will speak to the issue and share any reflections they may have.

Another issue we should consider is whether the total number of retired senior military officers selected for high-ranking positions in the Trump administration will impact the dynamic of the interagency process and the advice that the President receives. It is true that, throughout our history, retired general officers have often held positions at the highest levels of government as civilians. One notable example is General Colin Powell, when he ably served as Secretary of State under President George W. Bush.

What concerns me, however, is the number of retired senior military officers chosen to lead agencies critical to our national security and the cumulative effect it may have on our overall national security policy. In addition to General Mattis, General John Kelly has been nominated to lead the Department of Homeland Security, while General Michael Flynn will serve as the National Security Advisor, both of whom, like General Mattis, have retired from Active Duty service in the past few years.

While he is not a civilian and remains on Active Duty, if we include the Chairman of the Joint Chiefs of Staff, General Joseph Dunford, the leadership of our national security apparatus would be comprised of two retired four-star generals, one Active Duty four-star general, and one retired three-star general.

Now, diversity of opinion is important when crafting policy and making decisions as weighty as those facing the next administration. I think it is appropriate for the committee to consider the consequences that so many leaders with similar military backgrounds will have for the development of defense policy, the impact it could have on the civilian and military personnel serving in these organizations, and how it may shape the advice that will ultimately be provided to the President of the United States.

Finally, if Congress provides an exception for General Mattis, a question this committee must address is the precedent this action sets for such waivers in the future. The restriction was enacted into law for good reason. General George Marshall is the only retired military officer to receive this exception. I hope our witnesses will provide their assessment of this issue and if they believe providing an exception at this time opens the door to more waivers in the future. I personally believe such waivers would destroy the principle that is so critical to the central tenet of our civil-military relations. Congress is in a position where they are making a critical decision, and your advice would be deeply appreciated on this point, particularly.

I want to make it clear that I—concerns I've expressed are not a reflection on the personal attributes of General Mattis. General Mattis will testify before this committee later this week. I look forward to having a robust discussion on his record as well as his views on defense strategy and policy.

Additionally, it is not my belief that previous military service is a disqualifying factor for leading the Department of Defense. Nothing could be further from the truth. Many former members of the Armed Forces have served their country with distinctions as civilians after leaving the military service. One only has to look at many of my colleagues on this committee to appreciate how their prior military service has positively impacted their work in the Senate, and those who have served know better than most the sacrifices required to defend our Nation, including full-weighting consequences of making the decision to send our men and women in uniform into harm's way.

What this hearing is about is the principle of civilian control of the Armed Forces, the bedrock of civilian-military relations and one of the defining tenets of our democracy. We must protect against it being compromised or weakened. Any changes or waivers must be cautiously and carefully considered.

Again, I want to thank the Chairman for holding this hearing so that we can do just that. I look forward to the testimony of the witnesses.

Thank you, Mr. Chairman.

Chairman MCCAIN. Thank you.

Welcome, Dr. Hicks.

STATEMENT KATHLEEN H. HICKS, SENIOR VICE PRESIDENT; HENRY A. KISSINGER CHAIR; DIRECTOR, INTERNATIONAL SECURITY PROGRAM, CENTER FOR STRATEGIC AND INTERNATIONAL STUDIES

Dr. HICKS. Thank you, Chairman McCain, Ranking Member Reed, and distinguished members of the committee, for the invitation to appear before you today. Thank you also for taking the time to consider civilian control of the Armed Forces as it pertains to the nomination of James N. Mattis, U.S. Marine Corps, Retired, as Secretary of Defense.

The issue before you today regarding a possible exception to the limitation against appointment of persons within seven years of relief from Active Duty as a regular commissioned officer is one that has caused significant discussion within the national security community. We are blessed in the United States with a strong civil-military relations history. Tensions do exist, however, and we should never take for granted that civilian control of the military, nor healthy civil-military relations more generally, are a foregone conclusion for the Republic.

Congress's passage of the limitation on previously commissioned officers serving as Secretary of Defense within ten years of the cessation of their service, subsequently amended to seven years, has been one of the primary means employed to maintain civilian control. The Defense Secretary position is unique in our system. Other than the President acting as Commander in Chief, the Secretary of Defense is the only civilian official in the operational chain of command to the Armed Forces. Unlike the President, however, he or she is not an elected official. It is my view that the principle of excluding recently retired commissioned officers from serving as the Secretary of Defense is a prudent contribution to maintaining the constitutionally grounded principle of civilian control, both symbolically and in practice.

A permanent elimination or modification to this statute would be detrimental to the health of our civil-military relations and our national security. So, too, would be substantially populating the upper ranks of our national security structures with recently retired senior military personnel or Active Duty personnel well beyond those positions already designated in statute. I come to this conclusion based on a number of factors.

First, a regular reliance on former commissioned officers to serve as the Secretary of Defense or to widely populate the national security establishment's senior cadre would undermine the international security advantages that accrue to the United States from modeling strong civilian control. Others watch our behavior closely. They note that our leadership typically communicates through civilian channels, that our policymakers appear in civilian attire, and that our military demonstrates respect and deference to civilian leaders. It is also important to our citizens and those around the world that they witness a model in which senior civilians manifest appropriate approaches to civil-military relations demonstrated in their respect for the professionalism, sacrifice, and expertise of military personnel and in their knowledge of issues important to the profession of arms. These outward actions by our military and civilian officials support U.S. efforts to promote the embrace of freedom and democracy in the world, which reduces the instability, external aggression, and internal repression typically associated with military governments.

Second, were recently retired or Active Duty military officers routinely selected for Secretary of Defense or to widely populate senior civilian positions in government, it would risk furthering incentives for Active Duty officers to politicize their speech and/or actions and for civilians to seek to ascertain the political viewpoints of officers as part of the recruitment and hiring process for political positions.

This leads to a third concern, a coterie of individuals with like background typically accompanies a senior appointee into government. Academics know lots of academics. Economists know many economists. Former military personnel have extensive military networks. This is natural. But, what is unique in the national security world is the imperative for healthy civil-military relations. This requires guarding against an over-reliance on military viewpoints, just as it relies on ensuring those coming from civilian backgrounds act as respectful and knowledgeable counterparts.

Fourth, the United States has an interest in developing knowledge and expertise about the Armed Forces among those who have not served, especially in those who have not served at very senior levels. Motivating civilians to invest in careers in the defense sector requires having positions of meaning to which they can aspire. More generally, it requires validation that such career pathways are legitimate, that civilians can bring value, expertise, and perspectives to the defense enterprise.

Fifth, a recently retired senior officer at the helm of DOD risks prejudice with regard to service interests. Resources are always more constrained than one would like, so competition for dollars and mission space among the military departments is a constant reality. A Secretary of Defense who is closely associated with a particular service may find it difficult to be perceived as unbiased on important questions regarding service roles, combatant-command missions, and resource shares.

These reasons undergird the Congress's general prudence with regard to the limitation on commissioned officers recently relieved from Active Duty from assuming the position of Secretary of Defense and for this committee to remain vigilant to the possible negative effects of a broad representation of former senior officers in the national security cadre. I do not foresee imminent militarization of our national security architecture, but the concerns about civilian control that motivated our founders and the architects, the post-World War II security architecture, have continued validity. We should not risk a failure of imagination.

Despite all of these considerations, however, it is my personal conclusion that it is appropriate to create a specific exception to the statute for the Senate to consider the confirmation of General James N. Mattis. I reach the assessment based on two primary factors: the qualities of the specific nominee together with the safeguards in place to protect civilian control of the military in the presence of such an exception. Based on my professional interactions with General Mattis and a review of available material, I believe his recent retirement from military service should not be disqualifying to his consideration by this committee. I am persuaded not only by his grasp of the most important security issues our Nation faces, but also by his clear commitment to, and embodiment of, the principles of civilian control of the military. That commitment was evident in every interaction I had with General Mattis when I served as a senior—a civilian defense official, an experience shared by all such officials with whom I have spoken. His recently published work on civil-military relations reinforces my personal impressions.

The second reason I believe it is acceptable to make an exception to consider the President-elect's preferred nominee is that I assess that the state of U.S. civil-military relations to be strong enough to withstand any risks such a once-in-two-generations exception on its own could pose. The United States Congress, the Nation's statutes and courts, the professionalism of our Armed Forces, and the will of the people are all critical safeguards against any perceived attempts to fundamentally alter the quality of civilian control of the military in this country. Should an exception be made in this case and General Mattis be confirmed as Secretary of Defense, oversight by this and other committees will be critical in reassuring domestic and foreign audiences that civilian control of the military is alive and well in the United States of America.

As I stated earlier, I believe General Mattis's own behavior will reinforce that message. If it does not, this Congress and the courts of the United States should hold him accountable.

I would like to close with an important caveat to my endorsement for this exemption. I have grave concerns about the issuance of any exemption to section 103(a) of title 10 being portrayed or perceived as the result of the United States Senate agreeing with the President-elect that it is, quote, "time for a general," unquote, to serve as Secretary of Defense. It should never be considered "time for a general" to fill the senior-most non-elected civilian position in the operational chain of command. Rather, this exemption is about a particular individual who is well qualified for the position to which the President-elect has nominated him, the anticipation that the exemption will be a rare generational one, and an assessment that there is at this time a healthy appreciation of the principle for civilian control of the military in this country.

Although I would likely not agree with a Secretary Mattis on every major defense issue of the day, I am convinced that he passes the standard set forth during consideration of George Marshall's exemption for this position, whom the Washington Post referred to as "a truly authentic American in his respect for, and devotion to, our American system of government."

I have submitted a fuller written statement for the record.

Thank you.

[The prepared statement of Dr. Hicks follows:]

Prepared Statement by Kathleen H. Hicks

Chairman McCain, Ranking Member Reed, and distinguished members of the Committee, thank you for the invitation to appear before you today. I am grateful that you are taking the time to consider civilian control of the Armed Forces as it pertains to the nomination of General James N. Mattis, USMC (ret.) as Secretary of Defense. The issue before you today regarding a possible exception to the limitation against appointment of persons within seven years of relief from active duty as a regular commissioned officer is one that has caused significant reflection, discussion, and debate within the national security community. In the United States, we are blessed with a history of strong civil-military relations. Tensions do exist, however, and we should never take for granted that civilian control of the military, nor healthy civil-military relations more generally, are a foregone conclusion in our Republic.

The principle of civilian control of the military is at the core of the American civil-military dynamic. It is firmly grounded in our Constitution and cemented in hundreds of years of supporting statute, regulation, military education, training, and culture, and senior civilian practice. At the outset of the Republic, when concern was high over the threat that a standing military could pose, maintaining fairly limited federal forces helped ameliorate (though did not eliminate) those concerns. Two world wars and the emerging Cold War environment convinced Americans in the twentieth century that a more substantial standing Armed Forces was appropriate to secure U.S. interests. Yet many were wary that such a standing force could tempt militarization and the resulting despotism experienced in Germany and Japan. These competing imperatives created what Samuel Huntington called a "new conservatism" that attempted to balance civilian control with improved military readiness.

Congress's passage of the limitation on previously commissioned officers serving as Secretary of Defense within ten years of the cessation of their service (subsequently amended to seven years) has been one of the means employed to maintain civilian control despite the presence of a sizable standing force. Three years after enacting this measure, Congress created an exception to allow for the service of George C. Marshall as Secretary of Defense. No other such exception has been sought or granted until now.

The Defense Secretary position is unique in our system. Other than the President acting as commander in chief, the Secretary of Defense is the only civilian official in the operational chain of command to the Armed Forces. Unlike the President, however, he or she is not an elected official.

It is my view that there is a sound and enduring rationale for the principle of excluding recently retired commissioned officers from serving as the Secretary of Defense. It is not a limitation on these individuals' service in civilian positions in government, in national security, or even in the Department of Defense more generally. Indeed, veteran's preferences rightly help promote the federal service of former members of the Armed Forces. Rather, it is a narrowly targeted restriction for the one nonelected civilian position in the operational chain of command. As such, it is a prudent contribution to maintaining the constitutionally-grounded principle of civilian control, both symbolically and in practice, in the presence of a sizable and highly capable 21st century military.

A permanent elimination or modification to this statute would be detrimental to the health of our civil-military relations and our national security. So, too, would be substantially populating the upper ranks of our national security structures with recently retired senior military personnel, or active duty personnel well beyond those positions already designated in statute. I come to this conclusion based on a number of factors.

First, a regular reliance on former commissioned officers to serve as the Secretary of Defense, or to widely populate the national security establishment's senior cadre, would undermine the international security advantages that accrue to modeling strong civilian control of the military. What we do in this area matters in the world. Others watch our behavior closely. They note that our leadership typically communicates through civilian channels, that our policy makers appear in civilian attire, and that our military demonstrates respect and deference to civilian leaders. However, the burden of our model does not fall solely on the military. It is also important our citizens and those around the world witness a model in which senior civilians manifest appropriate approaches to civil-military relations, demonstrated in their respect for the professionalism, sacrifice, and expertise of military personnel and in their knowledge of issues important to the profession of arms. These outward actions by our military and civilian officials support U.S. efforts to promote the embrace of freedom and democracy in the world, which reduces the instability, external aggression, and internal repression typically associated with military governments.

Second, were recently retired or active duty military officers routinely selected for Secretary of Defense, or to widely populate senior civilian positions in government, it would risk furthering incentives for active duty officers to politicize their speech and/or actions and for civilians to seek to ascertain the political viewpoints of officers as part of the recruitment and hiring process for political positions. The civil-military dynamic at the highest levels of government is already challenging, where the professional military ethos to provide "best military advice" must be exercised in the inherently politicized and civilianized universe of foreign and security policy decision-making. The lines between civilian and military roles can be blurry in the policy world; furthering such tensions is unhelpful for threading the needle that our civil-military compact requires.

This leads to a third concern. A coterie of individuals with like-background typically accompanies a senior appointee into government. Academics know a lot of academics, economists know many economists, and former military personnel have an extensive military network. This is natural, and all officials must take pains to ensure they develop well-rounded teams. What is unique to the national security world, however, is the imperative for healthy civil-military relations. This requires guarding against an over-reliance on military viewpoints, just as it relies on ensuring those coming from civilian backgrounds act as respectful and knowledgeable counterparts, with expertise and responsibilities typically distinct from those of their military colleagues and subordinates.

Fourth, the United States has an interest in developing knowledge and expertise about the Armed Forces among those who have not served, especially in those who have not served at the senior-most levels. Motivating civilians to invest in careers in the defense sector requires having positions of meaning to which they can aspire. More generally, it requires validation that such career pathways are legitimate— that civilians can bring valued perspectives to the defense enterprise.

Fifth, a recently retired senior officer at the helm of DoD risks some prejudice with regard to service interests. Most of our secretaries of defense have had prior service backgrounds, and some amount of predisposition or at least disproportionate familiarity with one service over the others is not unusual. Nevertheless, a very senior, recently retired officer is far more likely to have had an important role in shaping that service's policies and budgets. Resources are always more constrained than one would like, so competition for dollars and mission-space among the Military Departments is a constant reality. A Secretary of Defense who is closely associated with a particular service may find it difficult to be perceived as unbiased on important questions regarding service roles, combatant command missions, and resource shares. Overcompensation on such issues is also a possibility against which to guard.

These reasons undergird the Congress's general prudence with regard to the limitation on commissioned officers recently relieved from active duty from assuming the position of Secretary of Defense, and for this Committee to remain vigilant to the possible negative effects of a broad representation of former senior officers in the national security cadre. I do not foresee imminent militarization of our national security architecture, but the concerns about civilian control that motivated our Founders and the architects of the post-World War Two security architecture, have continued validity. We should not risk a failure of imagination.

Despite all of these considerations, concerns, and cautions, however, it is my personal conclusion that it is appropriate to create a specific exception to the statute for the Senate to consider the confirmation of General James N. Mattis, USMC (ret.). I reach this assessment based on two primary factors: the qualities of the specific nominee and the safeguards in place to protect civilian control of the military in the presence of such an exception.

Based on my professional interactions with General Mattis and a review of available material, I believe General Mattis's recent retirement from military service should not be disqualifying to his consideration by this Committee and the United States Senate to be confirmed as the nation's next Secretary of Defense. I am persuaded not only by his expert grasp of the most important security issues our nation faces but also by his clear commitment to and embodiment of the principles of civilian control of the military. That commitment was evident in every interaction I had with General Mattis when I served as a senior civilian defense official, an experience shared by all such officials with whom I have spoken. His recently published work on civil-military relations reinforces my personal impressions. As he and co-author Kori Shake rightly stated in their 2016 work on this topic:

> "The president is elected to determine the amount of effort to direct toward a war and has the right to disregard the military's counsel. Military leaders lack the public mandate to make necessary trade-offs between, for example, security and civil liberties."

And

> "Our military ... understands better than do civilians that its high stature with the American public depends on respecting the prohibition on activism beyond the military sphere." [1]

The second reason I believe it is acceptable to make an exception to the limitation on recently separated officers in order to consider the President-elect's preferred nominee is that I assess the state of U.S. civil-military relations to be strong enough to withstand any risk such a once-in-two-generations exception, on its own, could pose. The United States Congress, the nation's statutes and courts, the professionalism of our Armed Forces, and the will of the people are critical safeguards against any perceived attempts to fundamentally alter the quality of civilian control of the military in this country. Should an exemption be made in this case, and General Mattis be confirmed as Secretary of Defense, oversight by this and other committees will play a critical role in reassuring domestic and foreign audiences that civilian control of the military is alive and well in the United States of America. As I stated earlier, I believe General Mattis's own behavior will reinforce that message. It if does not, this Congress and the courts of the United States should hold him accountable.

I would like to close with an important caveat to my endorsement for this exemption. I have grave concerns about the issuance of any exemption to section 103(a) of title 10 being portrayed or perceived as the result of the United States Senate agreeing with the President-elect that it is "time for a general" to serve as Secretary of Defense. [2] It should never be considered "time for a general" to fill the senior-most nonelected civilian position in the operational chain of command. Rather, this exemption is about a particular individual who is well qualified for the position to which the President-elect has nominated him, the anticipation that the exemption will be a rare, generational one, and that it comes at a time of healthy appreciation of the principle for civilian control of the military. Although I would likely not agree with a Secretary Mattis on every major defense issue of the day, I am convinced that he passes the standard set forth during consideration of George Marshall's exemption for this position, whom the Washington Post referred to as "a truly authentic American in his respect for and devotion to our American system of government." [3]

Thank you for the opportunity to testify today on this important issue, and I look forward to your questions.

Chairman McCain. Thank you, Doctor.

Dr. Cohen.

STATEMENT OF ELIOT A. COHEN, ROBERT E. OSGOOD PROFESSOR OF STRATEGIC STUDIES, JOHNS HOPKINS SCHOOL OF ADVANCED INTERNATIONAL STUDIES

Dr. Cohen. Thank you, Senator McCain. It's an honor to appear before you. I have a—I also have a written statement, which I'd like to submit for the record——

Chairman McCain. Without——

Dr. Cohen.—if I might.

---

[1] Kori Schake and Jim Mattis, "Ensuring a Civil-Military Connection," in Kori Schake and Jim Mattis, eds., *Warriors and Citizens: American Views of our Military* (Stanford: Hoover Institution Press, Stanford, CA, 2016), 299.

[2] Donald J. Trump, transcript of interview with the *New York Times,* November 23, 2016. Accessed at: *http://www.nytimes.com/2016/11/23/us/politics/trump-new-york-times-interview-transcript.html?smid=tw-nytimes&smtyp=cur&—r=0.*

[3] "Marshall as Secretary," *Washington Post,* 14 September 1950, 10.

Chairman MCCAIN. Without objection.

Dr. COHEN. I have to say, listening to my friend and colleague, Dr. Hicks, it is very striking to me that the two of us are, I think, pretty much in complete agreement. I'll be making a somewhat different set of arguments, but I find myself very much convinced by hers, and I share her views.

My bottom line on the issue of the day is simple. I strongly support the law that prohibits individuals that have—who have served in the military from becoming Secretary of Defense within seven years of leaving the service. At the same time, I favor an amendment to permit General Mattis to serve in that office despite having met that cooling-off period.

To explain these positions, let me begin with some basic propositions about our country's experience with civil-military relations. The principle of civilian control of the military—not collaboration with it, not mere direction of it, but civilian control—is central to the American experience since colonial times. The bill of particulars directed at King George III in the Declaration of Independence reads, among other things, that he has effected to render the military independent of, and superior to, the civil power. For a century before the Constitution, and certainly throughout the history of the Republic, firm civilian control has been a matter of American consensus challenged only on such rare occasions as the Truman-MacArthur controversy in 1951 and then resolved unambiguously in favor of civilian authority.

Some degree of civil-military tension has always existed in our country, and that is usually a good thing, a source of productive divergence of views about everything from strategy to internal administration. At times, the difference of views have been acrimonious, as, for example, during the famous standoffs between Abraham Lincoln and George McClellan during the Civil War, or in the late 1940s over the desegregation of the Armed Forces, or the dispute over ending the draft in the early 1970s. In these cases, the civilian political view properly and beneficially prevailed.

The practice embodied in the law of having a civilian Secretary of Defense stems from both that history and, I think, from four sets of concerns:

The first is that it reflects the notion that control over the largest bureaucracy in our government, with the largest budget, and with enormous power in many dimensions, including, potentially, over the lives of our own citizens, must rest with someone who represents the American citizenry, not a military elite, which, in the nature of things, is appropriately self-selected along military lines until the very top ranks.

Second, it stems from the belief that there is a breadth of view and perspective essential to running the military and making war that is not likely to be found in someone who has spent 30 or 40 years in uniform. The Armed Forces are what one sociologist has called "a total institution," comparable in some ways to the priesthood in the Catholic Church. A career of military service affects every feature of one's life, down to how one wears one's hair. Living in such an institution and removed from civil society throughout the prime of one's life can be a narrowing as well as a broadening experience, and it certainly leaves an indelible mark. It is one reason why, in a certain sense, generals never retire.

Third, having a recently retired general officer as Secretary of Defense poses all kinds of practical problems. Would they be inclined to favor the Joint Chiefs of Staff, military, over the Office of the Secretary of Defense, civilian? Would they be inclined to favor their own service over the others? Would they bypass the Chairman of the Joint Chiefs of Staff as the senior military advisor to the President? Would they allow the normal rivalries or close friendships of their military career to affect their position of civilian head of the Department? Even the appearance of such biases, let alone the reality, would make effective leadership of the Department of Defense difficult or indeed impossible.

Fourth, the Secretary of Defense is in many ways the chief interlocutor or bridge, if you will, between our Armed Forces and our society, the President being too busy and burdened with many other responsibilities. It is the Secretary of Defense who represents the concerns, values, and interests of the Armed Forces to politicians and to society. In turn, he or she guarantees that democratic values, attitudes, and needs will inform and shape the American military.

Furthermore, countries that have routinely installed generals as Ministers of War or Defense have often had deeply problematic patterns of civil-military relations and suffered military failure, as well. France and Germany in the late 19th and early 20th centuries, Japan during the 1930s and World War II are two—are examples of this. Such is the practice in recent years in Russia, as it was in the Soviet Union. Even democracies that have gone down this route have suffered from the politicization of the senior officer corps by the routine appointment of retired military figures to this top civilian position. A prime case is Israel, whose politics are often roiled by maneuvering among Active Duty and retired generals, a point that has been noticed by American generals familiar with that country and well documented by Israeli scholars.

The long question, therefore, makes eminent sense. But it was amended in September 1950 to allow for the appointment of General George C. Marshall as Secretary of Defense, for two reasons. The first had to do with the sense of national emergency. The Korean War had gone on for three bitter months. The Inchon landings were about to begin, and with them a bloody campaign to reunify the peninsula in the face of warnings of Chinese intervention. At the same time, the United States was sending four divisions to reinforce the two already in Europe, our first peacetime commitment of substantial Armed Forces abroad. War with the Soviet Union, which had, only a year before, detonated a nuclear weapon, seemed a real possibility. In that setting, and having lost confidence in Secretary of Defense Louis Johnson, President Truman correctly believed that he needed an exceptional leader for the relatively new Department of Defense. Truman had tremendous trust in Marshall because of the General's character and judgment, as well as the exceptional breadth of experience of a man who had after all been an important Secretary of State as well as one of the architects of the greatest coalition in military history.

Second—and this clearly influenced Congress as well as President Truman—was the desire to reassure the American people in extremely difficult times. American political leaders correctly believed that Marshall, a revered figure because of his monumental role as Chief of Staff during World War II, could do that. Congress, therefore, amended the law reluctantly, insisting that, by so doing, it was not creating a precedent, and advising that this not be repeated in the future.

I believe, however, that our current circumstances warrant taking this step a second time. I have known General Mattis for well over a decade. He is probably the most widely read and reflective officer I know. He is a writing general, too, as Dr. Hicks has pointed out, the coeditor of a recent important book on civil-military relations. More important than any of that, he has shown himself to be a man of exceptional character and judgment and exemplary commitment to legal and constitutional norms. I would trust him to conceive and execute policy as anyone on this committee would wish. He's not General Marshall, but he is, indeed, a man of similar integrity and soundness, and of very wide experience.

Much as I admire and respect him, however, I would not advocate this change were it not for two other aspects of the question. We face a world that may not be quite as dangerous as that of 1950, but has some deeply troubling similarities to it. We are waging our third war in Iraq in a generation. We are not close to ending the Afghan war. We face a contest with jihadi elements seeking to inflict violence and destroy regimes across broad swaths of the globe. We must deal with a rising China with hegemonic aspirations in Asia, a revanchist Russia that has committed blatant aggression against its neighbors and even interfered in our own elections, an Iran that has paused but not halted its drive for nuclear weapons and regional ascendancy. We will soon be looking at a North Korea that has built intercontinental ballistic missiles that can hit the United States with nuclear weapons. Ours is a very dangerous world that can tip into crisis with very little notice.

Yet, even this sense of danger would not bring me to the point of urging a revision of the law were it not for my concerns about the incoming administration. I have sharply criticized President Obama's policies, but my concerns pale in comparison with the sense of alarm I feel about the judgment and dispositions of the incoming White House team. In such a setting, there is no question in my mind that a Secretary Mattis would be a stabilizing and moderating force, preventing wildly stupid, dangerous, or illegal things from happening, and, over time, helping to steer American foreign and security policy in a sound and sensible direction.

Under these conditions, then, I urge you to amend the law to permit the appointment of General Mattis, but, at the same time, I urge you equally strongly to keep the law on the books, even restoring, if it seems proper to you, the ten year cooling-off period. The principle of civilian control of the military is precious and essential to our form of government. Making an exception twice in nearly 70 years while keeping the fundamental legislation intact and reaffirming the arguments behind it will not, in my judgment, threaten that principle, but, rather, reinforce it.

[The prepared statement of Dr. Cohen follows:]

PREPARED STATEMENT BY ELIOT A. COHEN

I appreciate the opportunity to appear before the Committee on this important topic. What follows reflects my views as both a scholar of civil-military relations, and my experience as a senior government official who routinely dealt with general and flag officers, and issues of war and peace. [1]

My bottom line on the issue of the day is simple. I strongly support the law that prohibits individuals who have served in the military from becoming Secretary of Defense within seven years of leaving the service. At the same time, I favor an amendment to permit General James Mattis, USMC (ret.) to serve in that office despite failing to meet the seven year cooling off period.

To explain these positions, let me begin with some basic propositions about our country's experience with civil-military relations.

The principle of civilian control of the military—not collaboration with it, as some have put it, or mere direction of it—is central to the American experience since colonial times. The bill of particulars directed at King George III in the Declaration of Independence reads, among other things, that "He has affected to render the Military independent of and superior to the Civil Power." For a century before the Constitution, and certainly throughout the history of the Republic, firm civilian control has been a matter of American consensus, challenged only on rare occasions such as the Truman-MacArthur controversy in 1951, and then resolved unambiguously in favor of civilian authority.

Some degree of civil-military tension has always existed in our country, and that has usually been a good thing—a source of productive divergence of views about everything from strategy to internal administration. At times the differences of view have been acrimonious as, for example, during the famous standoff between Abraham Lincoln and General George McClellan during the Civil War, or in the late 1940's turmoil over desegregation of the Armed Forces, or the dispute over ending the draft in the early 1970's. In these cases, the civilian political view properly and beneficially prevailed.

The firm practice, embodied in section 113 (a) of title 10 of the U.S. Code, of having a civilian Secretary of Defense stemmed from this history and these values. It embodies four sets of concerns:

First, it reflects the notion that control over the largest bureaucracy in our government, with the largest budget and with enormous power in many dimensions including potentially over the lives of our own citizens, must rest with someone who represents the American citizenry—not a military elite, which in the nature of things is appropriately self-selected, along military lines until the very top ranks.

Second, it stems from the belief that there is a breadth of view and perspective essential to running the military and making war that is not likely to be found in someone who has spent thirty or forty years in uniform. The Armed Forces are what one sociologist has called "a total institution," comparable to priesthood in the Catholic Church. A career of military service affects every feature of one's life, down to how one wears one's hair. Living in such an institution at a remove from civil society throughout the prime of one's life can be a narrowing as well as a broadening experience, and it leaves an indelible mark. It is one reason why, in a certain sense, generals never truly retire.

Third, having a recently retired general officer as Secretary of Defense poses all kinds of practical problems: would they be inclined to favor the Joint Chiefs of Staff (military) over the Office of the Secretary of Defense (civilian)? Would they be inclined to favor their own service over the others? Would they bypass the Chairman of the Joint Chiefs of Staff as the senior military adviser to the President? Would they allow the normal rivalries or close friendships of their military career to affect their position of civilian head of the department? Even the appearance of such biases, let alone their reality, would make effective leadership of the Department of Defense difficult or impossible.

Fourth, the Secretary of Defense is in many ways the chief interlocutor between the military and society, the President being too busy and burdened with many other responsibilities. It is he or she who represents the concerns, values and interests of the Armed Forces to politicians and to society. In turn, he or she guarantees that democratic values, attitudes and needs will inform and shape the American military.

---

[1] *Supreme Command: Soldiers, Statesmen, and Leadership in Wartime* (New York: Free Press, 2002) and more recently, *The Big Stick: The Limits of Soft Power and the Necessity of Military Force* (New York: Basic Books, 2017). From 2007–2008 I served as Counselor of the Department of State with particular responsibility for strategic issues, including the wars in Iraq and Afghanistan.

Furthermore, countries that have routinely installed generals as Ministers of War or Defense have often had problematic patterns of civil-military relations, and suffered military failures as well. France and Germany in the late nineteenth and early twentieth centuries and Japan during the 1930's and World War II are examples of this. Such is the practice in recent years in Russia, as it was in the Soviet Union. Even democracies who have gone down this route have suffered from the politicization of the senior officer corps by the routine appointment of retired military figures to this top civilian position. A prime case is Israel, whose politics are often roiled by maneuvering among active duty and retired generals—a point often noticed by American generals familiar with that country and well documented by Israeli scholars.[2]

The law in question, therefore, makes eminent sense. But it was amended in September 1950 to allow for the appointment of General George C. Marshall as Secretary of Defense for two reasons.

The first had to do with the sense of national emergency. The Korean war had gone on for three bitter months; the Inchon landings were about to begin and with them a bloody campaign to reunify the peninsula in the face of warnings of Chinese intervention. At the same time, the United States was sending four additional divisions to reinforce the two already in Europe—our first peacetime commitment of substantial Armed Forces abroad. War with the Soviet Union, which had only a year before stunned the world by testing a nuclear weapon, seemed a real possibility. In this setting, and having lost confidence in Secretary of Defense Louis Johnson, President Truman correctly believed that he needed an exceptional leader for the relatively new Department of Defense. Truman had tremendous trust in Marshall because of the general's character and judgment, as well as the exceptional breadth of experience of a man who had, after all, been an important Secretary of State as well as one of the architects of the greatest coalition in military history.

Second, and this clearly influenced Congress as well as President Truman, was the desire to reassure the American people in extremely difficult times. American political leaders correctly believed that General Marshall, a revered figure because of his monumental role as Chief of Staff of the Army during World War II could do that.

Congress therefore amended the law reluctantly, insisting that by so doing it was not creating a precedent, and advising that this not be repeated in the future. I believe, however, that our current circumstances warrant taking this extraordinary step a second time.

I have known General Mattis for over a decade. He is probably the most widely read and reflective officer I know. He is a writing general too, the co-editor of an important recent book on civil-military relations. More importantly, he has proven himself to be a man of exceptional character and judgment, and exemplary commitment to legal and Constitutional norms. I would trust him to conceive and execute policy as any of us would wish. He is not General Marshall—but he is indeed a man of similar integrity and soundness, and of very wide experience.

Much as I admire and respect him, however, I would not advocate this change were it not for two other aspects of the question. We face a world that may not be quite as dangerous as that of 1950, but has deeply troubling similarities to it. We are waging our third war in Iraq in a generation. We are not close to ending the Afghan war. We face a contest with jihadi elements seeking to inflict violence and destroy regimes across broad swathes of the globe. We must deal with a rising China with hegemonic aspirations in Asia; a revanchist Russia that has committed blatant aggression against its neighbors and even interfered in our elections; an Iran that has paused but not halted its drive for nuclear weapons and regional ascendancy. We will soon be looking at a North Korea that has built intercontinental ballistic missiles that can hit the United States with nuclear weapons. Ours is a dangerous world that could tip into crisis with very little notice.

Even this sense of danger, however, would not bring me to the point of urging a revision of the law were it not for my views of the incoming administration. I have sharply criticized President Obama's policies, but my concerns pale in comparison with the sense of alarm I feel about the judgment and dispositions of the incoming White House team. In such a setting, there is no question in my mind that a Secretary Mattis would be a stabilizing and moderating force, preventing wildly stupid,

---

[2] See the work of one of Israel's most thoughtful scholars of civil-military relations, Yoram Peri, *Generals in the Cabinet Room: How the Military Shapes Israeli Policy* (Washington, DC: United States Institute of Peace, 2006). By far the most successful of Israel's defense ministers—David Ben Gurion, founding father of the Israel Defense Forces—had minimal military experience.

dangerous, or illegal things from happening, and over time, helping to steer American foreign and security policy in a sound and sensible direction.

Under these conditions, then, I urge you to amend the law to permit the appointment of General Mattis—but at the same time I urge you equally strongly to keep the law on the books, even restoring, if it seems proper to you, the ten year cooling off period. The principle of civilian control of the military is precious, and essential to our form of government. Making an exception twice in nearly seventy years, while keeping the fundamental legislation intact and reaffirming the arguments behind it, will not, in my judgment, threaten that principle but rather reinforce it.

Chairman MCCAIN. Well, thank you both.

Both of you have known General Mattis for some period of time. Has he always—or, have you ever known him not to have the utmost commitment to the civilian control—our fundamental principle of civilian control of the military?

Dr. COHEN. I have always known him to have exactly that commitment.

Chairman MCCAIN. Dr. Hicks?

Dr. HICKS. Agree.

Chairman MCCAIN. I guess just one other comment or question. What you bring to mind, Dr. Cohen, is that, at least in the minds of some of us, the world is in greater danger than it's been since the days of then-General, slash, Secretary Marshall. There's very few people in—both in and out of the military that have the experience with these challenges that General Mattis does at this time. Would you agree?

Dr. COHEN. Yes, sir, I would agree, although I would just add that, as has long been pointed out, the Secretary of Defense is, other than the presidency, probably the most difficult job in the Federal Government. I would trust General Mattis as much as, or more than, just about anybody else. But, I do think the range of challenges he's—he will face, if he is confirmed, will be enormous.

Chairman MCCAIN. So, there is some historic parallel between the selection and need for General Marshall as there is today a need for the experience and knowledge and leadership of General Mattis. Is that—is it—do you agree with that assessment, Dr. Hicks?

Dr. HICKS. I—with the emphasis on the individual characteristics of General Mattis, I agree with that. I would hesitate to ever say, as I said, that there's any indication that dangerous times require a general. I don't think that's the issue. I think dangerous times require experience and commitment, which I think—as your question suggests—which I think General Mattis can bring.

Dr. COHEN. If I may, Senator, just to add to that. I don't think one can consider this case—rather somewhat unlike the case of 1950—without regard to the President. I mean, the President has to have somebody that they will listen to. I guess I do tend to believe that President-elect Trump will be inclined to listen to General Mattis. That, for me, is a very, very important consideration.

Chairman MCCAIN. One can only hope.

Senator Reed.

Senator REED. Well, thank you very much, Mr. Chairman.

Let me thank the witnesses for very thoughtful and eloquent testimony about a very significant issue.

Again, let me thank the Chairman for structuring this process so that we could have careful deliberation of the policy before we actually consider the legislation. Thank you very much, Mr. Chairman.

Dr. Hicks, you pointed out that this is a rare generational moment. I think, Dr. Cohen, you would agree also. That leads to a sort of very pragmatic question, if I may, that if, indeed, General Mattis is confirmed, but if he leaves office, that we would almost have to reflexively object to a replacement of another recently retired military officer. Would that be your view, Dr. Hicks?

Dr. HICKS. It would be. In fact, I think less a risk that this sets a new precedent, I think it's an opportunity cost. That is to say that I would not imagine, in the next 20-plus years, that we would see ourselves back in a hearing of this nature over another recently retired general officer.

Senator REED. Dr. Cohen, your thoughts?

Dr. COHEN. I very much agree with Dr. Hicks.

Senator REED. Thank you.

Dr. Cohen, you pointed out in your testimonies one of the areas of concern that I raised, which is a dynamic that results when a non-civilian is the head of the Department of Defense, which is— the principal military advisor to the President is the Chairman of the Joint Chiefs of Staff. Yet, you have two very competent—ironically, Marine four-stars, probably with at least tangential service, if not joint service. In—how do we avoid—or how would the—if General Mattis is confirmed, how does he consciously avoid that? How do we monitor—in fact, you both made the point, we have a role of making sure that this, if it takes place, is done aboveboard entirely, completely. Could you comment?

Dr. COHEN. Well, the first thing I would say is, absolutely, the role of congressional oversight, and particularly by this committee, I think—never be important than it's going to be in coming years. I first met General Dunford, actually, when he was General Mattis's Chief of Staff in Iraq, when General Mattis was commanding 1st Marine Division. I've—I know both of them reasonably well. I guess my feeling about that is, these are both men with a—an exceptional sense of professional ethics and rectitude. This will basically come down to relationships between two personalities. I think they will both be very conscious about what the lanes are that they operate in. But, there's no question, it will be challenging.

I guess the other point one will have to make is, it'll be interesting to see how long General Dunford is going to stay as the Chairman and who's the next Chairman. Presumably, it'll become a little bit easier. But, this will undoubtedly be an issue, and it would be the most natural thing in the world for a President Trump to ask General Mattis to act as kind of a military advisor. I think General Mattis will be—as Secretary Mattis—will be self-conscious enough to say, "You know, you really should be directing that question—I have my views, but you should be directing that question to the Chairman."

Senator REED. Let me ask you both, too. The Secretary of Defense has responsibilities strategic, but huge responsibilities when it comes to running a huge bureaucracy with all of the management issues and personnel issues and logistical issues and other issues. Your sense of this exemption in that context. Typically, a civilian going into this role would have great expertise in business or in other management positions within government. That's not the case. General Mattis has a complete dedication to the Marine Corps since—17 or so. So—Dr. Hicks first, and then Dr. Cohen.

Dr. HICKS. Well, I think it's fair to say every Secretary comes in truly with a unique set of skills. When you're staffing in and around that, not just in the national security team, but in the Defense Department, you do need to take account, absolutely, in the fuller staffing, the deputy position and others, what kind of management expertise is being brought in. I don't think it's fair to put every attribute of necessary management quality, international security experience, experience with the military or the Armed Forces, understanding of the bureaucratic elements—it's too much, really, to layer onto one person, but it's very important, as this committee looks at confirmations for the whole team for defense, that those attributes are covered.

Senator REED. Dr. Cohen, your comment.

Dr. COHEN. I completely agree with Dr. Hicks.

Senator REED. Thank you very much.

Thank you, Mr. Chairman.

Chairman McCAIN. Senator Inhofe.

Senator INHOFE. Thank you, Mr. Chairman.

It's rare that a confession like this is made, but I really did come here to learn. It's been really good testimony. I—one thing that has occurred to me is—we keep repeating over and over again that the senior—the senior officer. What about enlisted personnel?

Dr. COHEN. I think that's a completely different issue, Senator. I really do. I think there's—you know, I could give you a long lecture, which would bore you to tears, about the history of civil-military relations, but I think the distinction between officer and enlisted is quite important. But, more importantly, you know, the purpose of the law is really to exclude general officers from moving from——

Senator INHOFE. Yeah.

Dr. COHEN.—being generals to Secretaries.

Senator INHOFE. I understand that. The—of course, we had Chuck Hagel.

Do you have any thoughts about that, Dr. Hicks?

Dr. HICKS. I would just agree, it is very different. Secretary Hagel, coming as a former enlisted, really did bring——

Senator INHOFE. Lots of time, too.

Dr. HICKS. Yes. He brought a unique perspective in that sense, but it is unlike the idea of someone coming from the top of the organization, the military hierarchy, into the top of the civilian——

Senator INHOFE. Yes.

Dr. HICKS.—hierarchy.

Senator INHOFE. No, I understand that.

Dr. HICKS. So, it just has a different character.

Senator INHOFE. Okay. The—I understand that. That's——

Well, you know, each one of you talked about what would justify a—treating this differently than it's been treated since George Marshall. I—the only disagreement I would have—and I think that you come up from a much more learned perspective, but—when you made the statement that the sense of national emergency and—was not as dangerous as it was back in the '50s, I have a hard time with that one, because I look and see that—and I've often said that I look wistfully back at the days of the Cold War. But, right now, we have mentally deranged people who are developing a capability of inflicting huge damages on this country. That does——

So, whom do you—explain, just very briefly, when you say there's never a time for a general. Tell me what you mean by that.

Dr. HICKS. Sure. What I mean to say is, because of the way our Framers put forward civilian control of the military as central——

Senator INHOFE. Yeah.

Dr. HICKS.—President is Commander in Chief, always in a civilian capacity, even if the President, like Eisenhower, is a former general—in the same instance, the Secretary of Defense is a very unique position in our system. It's non-—it's—it also carries an operational chain-of-command responsibility, but is not nonelective, so there is special concern around it. My point being, that position may be filled with someone with military experience or not military experience. What we want to look for is someone who has the right desire for knowledge and expertise and judgment and character to live out the principles about Secretary of Defense issues. We don't pick them because they're a general officer. That is antithetical——

Senator INHOFE. That's clear.

Dr. HICKS.—to our very system.

Senator INHOFE. Yeah. That's clear.

Dr. COHEN. Senator, if I could just—the historian in me wants to point out—in 1950, people thought there was a serious possibility that World War III was just around the corner. You know, I don't think any of us really quite feel that as—and, although I agree with your basic assessment of where we are these days.

Senator INHOFE. Yeah, of capabilities that are out there that weren't there before. That's good. I appreciate very much and enjoyed your testimony.

Thank you, Mr. Chairman.

Chairman MCCAIN. Senator Gillibrand.

Senator GILLIBRAND. Thank you, Mr. Chairman and Ranking Member Reed, for hosting this hearing. I think this is such a critical discussion for our Nation.

Interestingly, both of you believe so deeply in civilian control, but not because of this President. That is a enormously weighty and serious statement that you both said.

Now, Dr. Hicks, you didn't define what your concerns were. You just said "the attributes of this President." Dr. Cohen, you were quite specific about the fears that you had on judgment. Can you please be specific that—why this enormous exception should be made because of the judgment of this President or the attributes of this President? Because you both made a very strong case about why civilian leadership is essential to our democracy and a very important provision of our Founding Fathers' concept for what our democracy would look like.

Dr. COHEN. As you may know, Senator, I was one of the ringleaders in these two letters by Republican national security experts that were very critical of then-candidate Trump. I will just mention one of the issues which is referred to in both of those letters, and that's the issue of torture. As a candidate, the President-elect indicated that he would be in favor of the ample use of torture, not only against suspected terrorists, but against their families. That's outrageous. It's illegal. It's profoundly immoral. I think a General Mattis—a Secretary Mattis would refuse to comply with that kind of order, and I think that's very important.

Dr. HICKS. Senator——

Senator GILLIBRAND. Excuse me. You just said that you believe the Secretary of Defense wouldn't comply with an order from the Commander in Chief?

Dr. COHEN. A Secretary of Defense should never comply with an illegal order from the Commander in Chief.

Senator GILLIBRAND. Dr. Hicks?

Dr. HICKS. Senator, I don't recall referring to the President-elect's attributes. I did make reference to the statement he has made about, "It's time for a general," which worries me greatly. I will say—so——

Senator GILLIBRAND. You said—your quote was "qualities of the nominee."

Dr. HICKS. I'm sorry, I don't think I have that in my statement.

Senator GILLIBRAND. I wrote it down.

Dr. HICKS. I apologize.

Okay. In any case, my view is that there ought to be a strong national security team at all times in any presidency. In this particular configuration that we have, as has already been mentioned, there's a number of retired general officers coming in. There's a seeming lack of attention to career diplomatic skills inside that mix. I have concerns about the way in which that whole apparatus will operate. I think General Mattis could be a very strong figure in that. It is clear, as Professor Cohen has indicated, that the President-elect, at least in one instance that we know of quite publicly, has listened, in a way that's very effective for civilian control, to the advice of General Mattis. This being with regard to reversing any kind of viewpoint on illegal torture.

So, my view is that he could play a very helpful role in this administration. I would like to think that we—were we sitting here with a different President-elect who had nominated General Mattis, I would nevertheless probably come to the same conclusion. I think our—we may different slightly on that. Because I think, again, our system is healthy enough, and you are able, as part of that system, to regulate it and oversee it. I believe that we are also looking at a person who has attributes that are on the level of Marshall's attributes for Secretary of Defense.

Senator GILLIBRAND. Okay. So, now let's focus on the points that you both make in your writings, that are very clear, about the importance of civilian control.

Dr. Cohen, you specifically talk about the unequal dialogue and how important it is to have the diversity of opinions in advising on national security, and that there's a push and a pull that results in better outcomes. Dr. Hicks, you talk about the importance of thinking through the full rage—range of implications—operational implications, strategic implications, pragmatic implications, meaning technical feasibility, dollars and cents, et cetera, and political elements. So, without the diversity of opinion, with this particular group of national security advisors, where do you think this committee will need to have vigilance because we have a blindspot? What diversity of opinion will now not be offered because we have such a high complement of extraordinary public servants, extraordinary generals with extraordinary capabilities, but—you've both outlined the importance, because of the diversity, and we now lack that. So, I need you to tell this committee where are the blindspots that we will need to be aggressively providing oversight?

Dr. COHEN. I would say, in addition to all the other things that you do, the question of strategy. What are we using our Armed Forces for? I mean, traditionally Congress spends a lot of time on the administration of the Department of Defense, acquisition, lots and lots of things. But, I think you also have an enormous role to play in examining, exploring, in some cases critiquing the way in which we use military power to achieve political ends. You've done that before. But, I think it will be particularly urgent in the period going ahead.

Dr. HICKS. Again, I think I would emphasis, more than anything, the diplomatic skillset and how that's going to play out. That's obviously an issue for State Department, but it is an issue within the Department of Defense, as well. There's a lot of defense-to-defense diplomacy that we rely upon. You know, short of the—of actual use of arms, we have a lot of alliances and partnerships that are important to maintain and sustain and push forward. I think that will be something to pay close attention to, particularly given the President-elect's statements during the campaign with regard to allies.

Chairman MCCAIN. I thank you, Dr. Cohen, for pointing out that the oath that is taken is to support and defend the Constitution of the United States, not to obey the orders of the President of the United States. There is a law against torture. No Secretary of Defense or officeholder should violate the law. That's what I would rely on General Mattis or any other Cabinet member or anyone in position of responsibility. Their first obligation is to obey the law.

Senator Fischer.

Senator FISCHER. Thank you, Mr. Chairman.

One issue that we have seen come up in this debate is the so-called militarization of foreign and national security policy decisions. I've heard some arguments that if we confirm General Mattis, we're going to continue that trend. So, I would ask both of you, first, Do you think there is a trend towards that?

Dr. COHEN. Let me—I'll—let me speak as a former diplomat. I was the counselor of the Department of State for several years. There is clearly an imbalance simply because of the size of the Department of Defense and the way our combatant commands operate. I don't think the presence of a Secretary Mattis at the head of the Department of Defense matters, one way or another. You know, it gets down to much more mundane things, like, when a combatant commander shows up, they've got an airplane, they've got, you know, spear carriers and people in a vast entourage. When an Assistant Secretary of State shows up, they are kind of poured out of the back of a United Airlines plane, and they are not in— on a plane that has the seal of the United States. It's not surprising that the locals look at that and say, "Okay, we know who matters. It's the General." I think it's those kinds of issues. You know, I'm not being facetious, actually. It sounds humorous, but I'm not being facetious. I have personally seen that happen in capitals around the world, and that is something that is worthy of your attention.

Senator FISCHER. But, those actions aren't really the result of any decision or any action taken by any senior military leader, are they? It's more of a perception that is out there, right?

Dr. COHEN. Yes and no. I mean, part of it—you know, a combatant commander has resources. A combatant commander can do things. They can move airplanes and people and supplies and so forth. So, there is built-in this kind of asymmetry to the advantage of the Department of Defense, which is not exercised in a malign way or with malign intent. It just is. You know, if you need relief— flood relief or something like that, State Department can't do a whole lot for you. Department of Defense can.

Senator FISCHER. Okay.

Dr. Hicks?

Dr. HICKS. I completely agree with Professor Cohen. I think if you layer onto that the high level of trust that the American public puts in the military, which I think is right, but it is much higher than at places in other parts of government, and you combine those things along with the alacrity of the system with regard to DOD [Department of Defense] funding, with regard to even authorization for DOD, which I think you all know is—runs quite smoothly every year compared to that for other agencies—it's sort of—it's a bias inside the system that we just have to watch for. It's not malign, necessarily, but it is something to be careful about.

Senator FISCHER. Dr. Cohen, you mentioned the word "imbalance." We've seen, recently, I think, centralized power within the White House—National Security Council and not the Pentagon. Yet, some would argue that confirming General Mattis is going to, I guess, in their view, continue a growing trend of military influence. How would you respond to that?

Dr. COHEN. I think, in this particular context, not so much. I think, in this—in the particular context of the incoming administration, the—it is entirely true, more power has gravitated to the White House, and more, actually, than I think is healthy. I think, because General Mattis is such a forceful character, and if the Senate decides to confirm Mr. Tillerson as Secretary of State, you will have powerful cabinet secretaries. I'm hoping that part of what will happen will be, we'll see a little bit more authority going back to the Departments, at the expense of a very controlling White House. So, I think it may work the other way, actually.

Senator FISCHER. Wouldn't that also reinforce what is the role of Congress? If we do have Secretaries who regain—Cabinet Secretaries who are able to regain that power that they are given, wouldn't that bring more transparency to the agency itself, but also to reinforce the role of Congress, when it comes to the larger debate of the duties of Congress, when you have a Cabinet Secretary who respects and values the responsibilities of oversight, of developing relationships with committees here in Congress, with coming before committees in Congress and being truthful and transparent and open about their needs?

Dr. COHEN. I would say, absolutely. Your ability to hold the people you've confirmed accountable is just absolutely indispensable to the functioning of our system of government. It's going to be more important than ever.

Senator FISCHER. A strong Secretary would do that.

Dr. COHEN. I believe so.

Senator FISCHER. Thank you, sir.

Thank you, Mr. Chairman.

Senator REED [presiding]. On behalf of Chairman McCain, let me recognize Senator Warren.

Senator WARREN. Thank you, Ranking Member. Thank you for urging us to have this hearing today.

We've spoken a great deal today about civilian control of the military in terms of the President and the Secretary of Defense, but I want to raise a broader question about the relationship between the military and our citizens as a whole which relates to this question about civilian control.

I come from a military family. All three of my brothers serve. But, this isn't as common as it used to be. It's been more than a generation since we've had massive mobilization on the scale of World War I and World War II and Vietnam. America has an extraordinary professional fighting force, the best the world has ever seen, but many people in our country are disconnected from our military. I think our founders would have been surprised by this development. They were deeply worried about our country getting tied up in foreign wars, and they were especially worried about a President using the military to increase his own fame and to perpetuate his own power. That is why Congress, not the President, retains important war powers. It's also why the founders expected citizens to pay for military engagements and to serve in the military.

Now, Dr. Hicks, I know you also recognize the extraordinary skill and professionalism of our military, but, when we think about civilian control of the military, are there consequences to having wide portions of the population that no longer have substantial ties to an active military?

Dr. HICKS. Senator Warren, I do think there are consequences. I think it's a distortion that can play out both positively, if you will, and negatively with regard to decisions about use of force. I would just say, if I had to pick just a few items to focus on, I am concerned that the lack of understanding of the long-term cost of conflict is exacerbated by individuals in the country being less familiar with the military. I think you see that play out, if you will, in the longer-term stabilization decisions we've had to make over time in the United States.

Senator WARREN. Thank you. You know, when—one of history's great military strategists, Carl von Clausewitz, talked about warfare, he noted the need to pay attention not only to the military and to political leaders, but also to the people of the Nation. So, I want to ask a related question about public support for decisions about when to use our military.

If we want to be successful in future wars, do you think we need to develop a strategy to get citizens more engaged? If so, why? Dr. Hicks? Dr. Cohen? Whoever would like to on this.

Dr. HICKS. I do think we're facing a crisis on civic engagement on foreign and security policy. We have seen, over time, a general consensus about what the U.S. role in the world is fraying—not breaking, but fraying—and there seems to be a lot of confusion and uncertainty. As a matter of fact, two of the most recent major polls of the public on foreign and security policy, the Pew Poll and the Chicago Council [on Global Affairs] poll, use "uncertainty" in their titles. It just goes to this idea that the public and the elite, if you will, no longer are having a constant dialogue about what the U.S. role is in the world.

Senator WARREN. Thank you.

Dr. Cohen, would you like to add anything to——

Dr. COHEN. Yes, I would.

First thing, to that immediate point, I would say, in my view, it is extremely important that Congress authorize the use of military force. I was deeply disappointed that, for our third Iraq war and for the Libyan intervention, that did not occur. I'm not going to assign blame, I'm just saying, as a citizen, I found that profoundly disappointing.

To your earlier point, I would say that there are a number of things that you can do, that we should do. One is simply—and I'm—by the way, I speak as the father of two servicemembers—the first is to get ROTC [Reserve Officers' Training Corps] programs out on all kinds of campuses, including campuses where they are not—have not traditionally been. We're both from Massachusetts, so we know what we're talking about there. Even if it's not entirely efficient, to have ROTC out there as a presence.

I also have to say that I think that a lot of the attempt to rationalize our base structure didn't help us in this regard. Again, I'll speak as somebody from Massachusetts. When I was in ROTC, we were always at Fort Devins, trampling around in the mud. There was a military presence in New England. There's much less of a military presence today. That's not healthy. Even if it's not entirely administratively rational or economically rational, I think it is very important for people to have contact with the military. For a number of reasons, one of which is, it's also I'm sorry not to put the military on too much of a pedestal. You know, Harry Truman was a great President because he had been a National Guard captain, and he knew the underside as well as the things that are truly noble and inspiring about the military and about military service.

So, I really worry about it, from—if you will, from both ends.

Senator WARREN. Well, I just want to say thank you very much. You know, it seems to me that the broader divide between our citizens and our military makes it even more important that we continue to keep front and center the importance of having civilian control over the military.

Thank you.

Thank you, Mr. Chairman.

Senator REED. On behalf of Chairman McCain, let me recognize Senator Ernst.

Senator ERNST. Thank you, Mr. Chair.

Thank you both today. This has been a very, very enlightening hearing, so I appreciate your testimony.

Dr. Cohen, thank you for your support of ROTC programs. As a proud member of the Cyclone Battalion from Iowa State, I thank you for that. I do believe that we need more of those programs in other areas that aren't maybe as widely accepting today. So, thank you very much for that.

While I still do have many commitments to garner from retired General Mattis before I affirm that I will be supporting him for Secretary of Defense, I strongly believe he understands and respects the importance of civilian control of our armed services. I retired just a little over a year ago from the military, and I do consider myself a civilian. I view retired General Mattis as a civilian also.

Dr. Cohen, in your written statement, you suggested that Congress confirmed George Marshall because the United States faced imminent and substantial national security threats requiring his expertise. You drew a parallel between things that are ongoing today. We have North Korea, we have Russia, China, radical Islamic terrorism. What I want to do is add to that list. I would also include there a hollowed-out military, which is what I believe that we have right now. As a result of Obama administration policies, our Army has fewer soldiers, and our Navy has fewer ships, our Air Force is flying antiquated aircraft. U.S. servicemembers, while proud, are understandably anxious. Do you see the need for a strong soldier statesman such as—for Secretary of Defense—just like we did in the 1950s? If so, does James Mattis, like George Marshall, really fit into that mold?

Dr. COHEN. You know, I'm—again, I'll just speak as an historian. The buildup of the 1950s was not the work of one individual. It was a whole team of quite exceptional public servants and great presidential leadership, as well. But, I would say that I completely agree with your assessment of the situation. I've, in fact, just written a book on the subject. I think there is a need for what will probably be a fairly substantial expansion in military spending, because we're facing quite—a quite diverse set of challenges, perhaps none of them as overwhelming as the possibility of a third world war—in this case, with the Soviet Union—but our forces are not adequate for that right now. So, this is partly going to be an issue of resources, but it will partly be the nature of the team that is then created to supervise a substantial increase in defense spending.

Senator ERNST. Okay.

Dr. Hicks, anything to add to that?

Dr. HICKS. Well, I would just say, I agree that General Mattis, if confirmed as Secretary of Defense, could be a very effective spokesperson for the requirements of the military. Again, to my prior answer to Senator Warren on the issue of what's the U.S. role in the world, we clearly have a gap between the perception of what we want to be able to achieve in the world and what we're willing to put toward it and what it requires. I think the strategic man inside General Mattis, if a Secretary Mattis, would come forward to help us close that gap, which I think many of us would greatly appreciate.

Senator ERNST. Thank you.

Dr. Hicks, you concluded in your statement that it is appropriate to create a specific exemption, a once-in-a-70 year exception to the law for this nominee based on his unique qualifications and because of the safeguards in place to protect civilian control of the military. You state that the ultimate safeguard is the United States Congress. I agree with that assessment. But, in light of that, what commitments should we garner from General Mattis in order to ensure that we are doing our part and our due diligence in vetting him for the position of Secretary of Defense?

Dr. HICKS. I think, first and foremost, is the comment that came up earlier in the discussion about adhering to the Constitution of the United States, not to any individual President or other political official. I think that is first and foremost. When General Marshall served as Secretary of Defense, it was well prior, of course, to Goldwater-Nichols, but it was prior to having a truly strong Chairman of the Joint Chiefs of Staff. In statute, I think securing and understanding of how he would look at this pretty unique situation of a recently retired four-star, and what has been strengthened over time as a very centrally powerful Chairman of the Joint Chiefs of Staff, how that would operate. Again, that he's always bringing his best judgment without bias to his prior Marine allegiance, if you will. I know a Marine is always a Marine. That would be very important, in my mind, as well.

Senator ERNST. Very good. Thank you very much, both of you.

Thank you, Mr. Chair.

Chairman MCCAIN [presiding], Senator Kaine.

Senator KAINE. Thank you, Mr. Chair.

Thanks, to the witnesses.

Dr. Cohen, you mentioned, just a second ago, that you believe, based on the current array of challenges in the world, we may need an expansion of military spending. I assume you believe that the arbitrary budget sequester that has put a cap on defense spending as well as nondefense discretionary spending is not smart.

Dr. COHEN. I would say I share the Chairman's view of sequester.

Senator KAINE. Great. Thank you. That view is well known to the members of the committee and shared on a——

Dr. COHEN. That's why I put it that way.

Senator KAINE.—shared on a bipartisan——

Chairman MCCAIN. This is——

Senator KAINE.—view.

Chairman MCCAIN. This is an R-rated hearing.

[Laughter.]

Senator KAINE. Two items. The title of the hearing is not just about the waiver for General Mattis, it's testimony on civilian control of the Armed Forces. To touch upon two points that have already been raised, civilian control over our Armed Forces is throughout the Constitution in different ways, not just the notion of this waiver, which is not constitutional, but statutory, the requirement that we're talking about, but also the role of Congress in warmaking powers in article 1. You referred to this a second ago, Dr. Cohen. In a book retrospect, the former Secretary of Defense Robert McNamara said this about the Gulf of Tonkin Resolution, "We failed to draw Congress and the American people into a full and frank discussion and debate of the pros and cons of a large-scale military involvement in Southeast Asia. It wasn't that we didn't have formal authority. We did. The problem wasn't with formalities. The problem was the substance." Neither the Congress nor the President intended that those words would be used as we used them. We're in the 15th year of using a 60-word authorization passed in the aftermath of the attack of 9/11, stretching it far beyond probably what was the original intent in a Congress that is nearly 70 percent people who weren't even here to vote on that authorization. You talked about your concern about the absence of an authorization for current military operations. Isn't the congressional warmaking power, the article 1 power that gives that decision to the people's elected legislative body, part of the framework of civilian control that we are obligated to uphold?

Dr. COHEN. Senator, I think you're absolutely right. There are many different aspects of civilian control that—to the—to include the fact that the President is the Commander in Chief, which is different than other countries do it. I completely agree with you on authorizations for the use of military force. I think—without wishing in any way to be critical of Congress, I think in—on some occasions, it's also been a way of avoiding responsibility. It—there's a requirement for Congress to step up and say, "I'm going to vote yea or nay on something like that." I also think one has to have a certain acceptance of the fact that you're going to authorize the use of force and then there's a limited extent to which you can predict the way that things are going to go.

But, that was also why I was, in response, I think, to Senator Gillibrand earlier, I said, "It's not just the vote about the authorization of the use of military force, it's also, you know, over—looking at strategy, getting those kinds of discussions going." I think that is one of the things I would hope you would ask General Mattis about, because I do think you should be part of that discussion. You're not going to be in the chain of command, but you should be part of that discussion.

Senator KAINE. Dr. Hicks, any additional comments on that?

Dr. HICKS. I would just agree completely with regard to the important oversight role of Congress, and specifically with regard to declarations of war and authorization for the use of military force. I want to thank you personally for how much you have invested in this issue, which I'm sure seems Sysphean at times. But, I really do hope, in this Congress, that there can be movement forward on a new authorization for these——

Senator KAINE. Multiple years of effort, I think I've managed to persuade two or three people on this, but I'm going to keep trying, because I think it matters.

[Laughter.]

Senator KAINE. It matters.

A second issue dealing with civilian control—and this touches upon questions that Senator Fischer asked—is the role of congressional oversight—budgetary oversight, the confirmation of a Secretary of Defense. We did some reforms in the most recent NDAA [National Defense Authorization Act] to reduce the size of the NSC [National Security Council] operation. We don't confirm the National Security Advisor. We have less oversight over the NSC operation as we do over the—a Secretary of Defense and a Pentagon. I actually would like each of you to comment upon the relationship between the NS—National Security Advisor and the NSC and the Secretary of Defense and what you think the right balance in that relationship should be in connection with this question of maintaining appropriate civilian control through the civilian elected Congress over military operations.

Dr. COHEN. You know, I would just say that this is really one of the most delicate and complicated questions of this kind one can deal with. So, I suppose my position would be, first, that, you know, the President really does deserve to have the staff that he or she wants, who are organized in the way that suits him or her best, and that they think are most effective.

Secondly, I have my own views about how a—having seen a bunch of National Security Advisors up close, there's a certain way that they should do their business, that they should not be understood to be principals, in the sense that a Cabinet Secretary is. The NSC staff should not be operational. It is largely a coordinating function. It is staffing the President of the United States. I think there may be something more to be gained by making sure that the functions of the NSC staff, rather than its particular size and so forth, are appropriate. I mean, I get very anxious when National Security Council staffers begin negotiating treaties with other countries. Again, speaking as an old State Department guy, that's really wrong. That should not happen.

Chairman MCCAIN. Not only negotiating, but deciding rules of engagement in faraway places.

Senator Kaine, I appreciate very much your advocacy on this whole issue, that you have been, sometimes, a voice in the wilderness, but you've also been absolutely correct. I know Senator Reed would like to work with you. Perhaps one of the ways to try to address this issue would be to have a hearing or two on this issue. Because, certainly, Congress has not exercised its responsibilities in conflicts that are going on throughout the globe. So, I thank you for raising that issue. I thank you for your continued tenacity. I want to commit to us making this a priority for this committee in the coming year.

Senator KAINE. I appreciate that, Mr. Chairman.

Chairman MCCAIN. I thank you.

Senator Perdue.

Senator PERDUE. Thank you, Mr. Chairman.

I agree with both of you in your testimony and comments so far in preparation for today. I think this is an extremely important tenet, one that we should strive to uphold, going forward. Any exception to it should be taken very, very seriously. So, I appreciate your comments on that.

Having said that, I agree with you, also, that I think we're facing a very unique and dangerous global security crisis today. I can't compare it to 1950. It's different. They didn't have cyberwarfare back then. They didn't have a nuclear North Korea. They didn't have an arms race in space. I think the need for integration between diplomacy and development and military capability has never been greater or more complicated. Because of that unique circumstance, I think, like General Marshall, General Mattis offers us a unique combination of skillsets and mindsets that make him an ideal candidate for right now, with certain cautions that you both have laid out.

Having said that, and having broad experience from the Foreign Relations Committee here, I'm very concerned about the relationship between diplomacy and development debates inside the Cabinet room between two military officers when it's a military option or a diplomatic option. Could you both speak to that with your personal experience of General Mattis?

Dr. Hicks?

Dr. HICKS. I'll begin.

I think you're right to have that concern, particularly, if I may, on development. It—the last 15 years of war, I think, have brought home, more than ever before, to members of the military the importance of development, or the role—maybe more precisely said, the role it plays. But, your average officer, I think, still maybe doesn't fully understand the role of USAID, in particular.

That said, I do think General Mattis, through his—both his role—well, his variety of roles, but particularly the roles as the head of U.S. then-Joint Forces Command, looking broadly at the future and at the integration of the military with other instruments of power, and, of course, as the Commander of U.S. Central Command, where a region, like many others, where you absolutely have to understand how these pieces integrate together, is critical. I think he will have a deep appreciation of the need for development and diplomacy experts that are nonmilitary.

Dr. COHEN. I guess I would have a couple of thoughts.

The first is that, it seems to me it's very rare that one has a choice between a military and a diplomatic option. The choice is much more likely to be diplomacy of one kind, backed by a military option, or diplomacy of a different kind, maybe not backed by a military option. Therefore, what matters most is actually the cooperation between the State Department and the Defense Department.

I was very privileged to serve, along with Senator Sullivan, under Secretary Rice, and to see the exceptionally close relationship that she had with Secretary Gates as Secretary of Defense. You know, anybody who is in an administration tends to feel that way, but I thought I was seeing an exceptionally close integration of diplomacy and military power. I think that's really the model. So, I think the question might be more to General Mattis, if he's Secretary Mattis, with the Secretary of State.

Senator PERDUE. Dr. Cohen, you had mentioned that, you know, we're not the first ones to do this as a country. I mean, certain countries have done this, historically, and some not so very well. You've called that out in your writings. Would you relate to us just a little bit about the cautionary comments that you've made about that, relative to other people's experience, other countries' experience with doing what we're talking about doing today, but also talk about the unique character of Dr. Mattis and why this might be a unique situation?

Dr. COHEN. Well, let me start with General Mattis. I—for me, what I find myself focusing on is not just the experience and the expertise, and so on; it is fundamentally my judgment about his character and his judgment. That's why I think it's very unfortunate people have used the phrase "Mad Dog." I've never heard anybody in the uniformed military refer to him as that. That is not what he is like. This is an extremely thoughtful, careful, prudent man. I think that's—that is a tremendously important thing.

To speak to the history of civil-military relations, the fact is, say, if you look at the French or the Germans, or even the Russians, the—when you begin to have retired generals as Ministers of Defense or Ministers of War, you are setting up the kinds of tensions and problems and blurring that we talked about, and the kind of isolation of the military from normal politics. In some ways, this is what has happened in Israel, which is probably, for us, the most interesting case, because it is a liberal democracy. But, I know that country pretty well. There is a serious problem with the politicization of the senior officer corps, there is a serious problem in distinguishing between the military advice of the serving Chiefs of the General Staff and a Minister of Defense, who, only a couple of years before, was a general officer. In fact, what's interesting is, the Israelis are—have introduced, and they've actually recently increased, their own time gap between when you can take off the uniform, when you can run for public office and serve in those kinds of positions.

Senator PERDUE. Thank you, Mr. Chairman.

Chairman MCCAIN. Senator Peters, welcome again to the committee.

Senator PETERS. Thank you, Chairman McCain. It's a pleasure to be here and to serve.

I'd thank our witnesses today for your testimony, both Dr. Hicks and Dr. Cohen. Thank you for addressing this very serious issue.

Just to pick up on Senator Perdue's comments about the need to make sure we're balancing military options with diplomatic, economic, the full range of power that can be projected around the world—soft power in addition to hard power—I think it's important to remember the last time we did grant this waiver, the—General Marshall, the—in addition to his extensive military experience, also served as a Special Envoy to China, was the Secretary of State and president of the American Red Cross. So, quite a diverse background, something that we're not looking at right now, despite all of the qualifications of General Mattis, but certainly a very rounded background, going into that position.

But, I'd like to turn to the book that General Mattis edited, which I think both of you have referenced. In that book, "Warriors and Citizens," he has a chapter from Dr. Thomas Owens, who's a professor at the Institute of World Politics. It's entitled, "Is Civilian Control of the Military Still an Issue?" which raises the prospect if that's even something we should be thinking about.

Dr. Owens writes that civil-military relations can be seen as a bargain. I'm going to quote from his writing here, "There are three parts to the bargain: the American people, the government, and the military establishment. Periodically, the civil-military bargain must be renegotiated to take into account political, social, technological, or geopolitical changes."

So, my question to both of you, first, is, Do you agree with that assessment, that, basically, as we're discussing the civil-military relations, that this is, basically, a bargain between the people, the government, and the military?

Dr. COHEN. No, I do not.

Senator PETERS. Why is that?

Dr. COHEN. Because the principle is civilian control of the military, full stop.

Senator PETERS. Ms.——

Dr. HICKS. I agree with that. I do think there is this issue of how, exactly, it manifests, again, in any given environment. An example would be that the particular statute that we're discussing now did not arise until 1947. I think, in large part, it arose—and there are a variety of reasons, but a large reason it arose is because we had come out of two world wars, we had seen militarized societies and their effects, and we were facing the prospect, which we still have, of a much larger and very capable standing military. The exact structure of how we operationalize civil-military relations changed in that context.

I do think that has been true throughout the history of the United States, of course, which is, we maintain the principle, and the particular way—just as this waiver would be, the particular way in which we judge what it requires to be healthy at a given time is assessed at that time.

Dr. COHEN. If I could, you know, the patterns clearly do change, but the word that I would really push back at is "bargain," as if it's a deal that gets cut between different segments of society. I think that's not the way our Constitution was intended to operate.

Senator PETERS. Well, thank you.

Later in his book—and this—that—the quote that I had was from a different author; it wasn't General Mattis—later in his book, General Mattis writes—and I'd love to have your comments on his thoughts on this issue—he writes, "If there is a contemporary departure from the American norm, it is that military commanders are more, not less, hemmed in by political leaders, because the wars we are fighting are more removed from everyday experience of most Americans." He goes on to say—this is his writing again, quote, "The combined effect is worrying, since elites without military experience alienated from the advice offered by the military are more likely to use military force ineffectively. We believe we have been seeing exactly this in American national security policies over the last dozen years."

Your response, please.

Dr. COHEN. I'm not sure I would agree with that. I mean, I understand it as a point of view. I think there has undoubtedly been a fair amount of friction, particularly in the last eight years, but there was friction in the—during the Bush administration, as well.

I think, you know, sometimes people like to think that there was a halcyon period, where generals and politicians got along very well. There wasn't. Again, I'm essentially a military historian. I can give you chapter and verse on that if you like. I—we—that is why I said in my statement that a certain amount of tension is the norm and is actually a healthy thing. But, I don't think I really, fully believe that.

I mean, look, the biggest 20th-century blowup in our civil-military relations was between President Truman and General Mac-

Arthur. President Truman had an outstanding war record in the first World War as a National Guard battery commander.

I would like to add just one thing. Having edited a bunch of books, I've stopped doing it, because you can't really control what the people in the book are going to say. I'd rather just say what I'm going to say. So, I wouldn't hang General Mattis with what some feckless author has put in there. You—it's—you have much less control than you might think.

Senator PETERS. Well, but let me be clear, the last two quotes that I read were General Mattis.

Dr. COHEN. Yes. No, I understand. I was——

Senator PETERS. Right.

Dr. COHEN.—referring to the previous quote.

Senator PETERS. The previous one, right.

Dr. HICKS. I, basically, agree with Professor Cohen. I would simply say, again, it's always hard to take quotes and assess them, but my recollection of that portion of his essay with his coauthor, Kori Schake, was—the context was also about this issue, again, of the societal removal, the one percent issue. I do think, again, it—that has effects. It distorts how we think, sometimes, about military force. It doesn't mean it's more likely we use it, which I think is more the implication, perhaps, of that passage, or we're less likely to use it. I do think it means that the more distant citizens become from their understanding of, if you will, the profession of arms, the more dangerous that is for us, because we remove ourselves from very real understanding of what the implications of use of force are.

Dr. COHEN. If I could, you know, there—I think there are other sources of tension, as well. People may conflate them. So, for example, simply the fact that anything that happens is instantaneously visible around the world—and when I'm—say "visible," I mean on YouTube—and, therefore, is a big deal, does mean that there's going to be more political attention. So, when you have an Abu Ghraib, it's not something that comes out, you know, a long time later and there are no photographs; it's right there in front of you, and it has real repercussions.

I also think some of this has to do with the nature of the particular wars that we've been fighting, which, in a variety of ways, are—have been conducive to civil-military tension. So, I think—I may agree with the diagnosis of the phenomenon. I might have a somewhat different analysis of some of the causes.

Senator PETERS. Thank you.

Chairman MCCAIN. You've exceeded your time, Senator Peters.

Senator Rounds.

Senator ROUNDS. Thank you, Mr. Chairman.

Part of the discussion earlier had to do with whether or not we were losing contact between the civilian and military members. I would just suggest that there are some areas where I just don't believe that that has happened. One area is with regard to the National Guard. All you have to do is to attend a single deployment ceremony or a welcome home ceremony or a funeral and you'll see that, when you mobilize the National Guard, you mobilize the entire community, and there is clearly a connection there which has not faded.

I think one thing that leads to that is, is that—that very, very close connection, where these folks are maintaining their relationship with their families and with that community, and folks see them actively involved, but they also see the sacrifice of the family, as well. Sometimes I suspect that our military members that have family back here, that sacrifice that those families make is probably not as evident in their local communities as it is when you recognize the Guard.

Let me just ask a just a couple of quick questions. I don't mean to split hairs, but we've talked a lot about the comparisons between General Marshall and General Mattis, and about the connectivity between the two, the similarities and so forth. Can I ask about what you see as the differences between the recommendation—the nomination at that time and the nomination that we have before us to date—the differences that, in your study and your review, that you've found, that you would point out to us.

Dr. COHEN. Before I do that, let me just—on your point about the National Guard, I completely agree, but I think there are many dimensions to that issue, and it's—seems to me it would be a good thing for our country if our business leaders, our academic leaders, our leaders of nonprofits also had family members or people that they knew who were serving, and that has other kinds of implications for how we go about recruiting people.

There are a number of differences. Obviously, General Marshall had—his military experience is different. He had—he was not a combat commander, as General Mattis most definitely has been. He was one of the masterminds of this great coalition effort. He had served as Secretary of State. I think that's tremendously important. A very effective Secretary of State for two years.

Conversely, I think one does have to point out, General Marshall was quite a sick man when the waiver was made. I think historians think that he was an extraordinarily effective Secretary of Defense, partly—I believe he had lost a kidney by then. He was in for about—he was in for about a year. So, General Mattis, I think, is a much more vigorous type, and that's actually nontrivial, I believe.

So, those, it would seem to me, would be the largest differences that you're dealing with. You know, General Marshall, finally, did have—he had one enormous challenge. That was, of course, dealing with General MacArthur with—whom he did not like, but who he tended to respect as the guy who was in charge out in the Far East. MacArthur was a very different kind of problem that—Mattis is not going to face any MacArthurs out there.

Dr. HICKS. I would add just two other factors. One relates to what Eliot just said, that, you know, he—he served a very short period of time. In fact, it—all evidence points to the fact that that was a prearranged agreement, that he would only serve for a limited period of time. He was essentially helping the President out, if you will, in a case where he had, I think, as you referenced earlier, a Secretary of Defense who was not working out for him. So, this was a way to transition with a very popular—politically, publicly popular figure, in the case of General Marshall. You can parse how much of that is similar and different in this case, but it is the fact that it wasn't his out-of-the-gate Secretary of Defense, it was a—more of a transitional approach.

The other thing I think bears in—repeating is that General Marshall, as best I recall, had come out—he had gone back into an Active Duty an status, so he was extremely recently retired just before taking on the position.

Dr. COHEN. He was actually technically not retired, because the way it worked, if you're a five-star general, which is what he was, was that you never retire. So, a lot of the discussion and the testimony is about, What do we do about his pay? I mean, what—the lofty issues were addressed, too, but some of it was pretty mundane.

Senator ROUNDS. Thank you, Mr. Chairman.

Chairman McCAIN. Senator King.

Senator KING. Thank you, Mr. Chairman.

Dr. Cohen, first, you mentioned a few minutes ago that you were reluctant to be critical of Congress. I don't know why you alone, among all the citizens of this country, should feel any reservations on that front.

[Laughter.]

Senator KING. I would suggest that—yes, that's right.

I also have to point out—a statement was made earlier about President Obama eviscerating the military or hollowing out the military. Again, this was—the budgets for the military come out of this body, and we impose limitations that the President's budgets reflect. So, again, I think we don't want to avoid responsibility for our role, either historically or on a going-forward basis.

The other point, it seems to me probably one of the greatest challenges to civilian control of the military occurred in the election of 1864, when George McClellan, one of the leading generals of the Union Army, ran against the President of the United States. Lincoln, himself, wrote his wife, in August of that year, saying he was likely to lose that election, and probably would have, other than for Sherman's taking of Atlanta in September, shortly before the election. I apologize to the Senator from Georgia for raising that difficult point.

[Laughter.]

Senator KING. When I was a small-town lawyer in Maine, one of the principles we used to discuss was, "Hard cases make bad law." Cases that are very appealing on the merits that—widows and orphans and other kinds of difficult issues, you end up creating precedents that are bad law. That's what I'm struggling with in this case. I think that's exactly what we're talking about here.

I have decided to support this amendment, because I don't think it will make bad law, because of the narrow way that it's drafted. I think it's important—we haven't discussed the specific language, but the language is, "This section applies only to the first person appointed as Secretary of Defense as described in subsection (a) after the date of this Act, and to no other person." That means it can't even be used by another appointment of this President. It is an extremely narrow precedent. The precedent was broken, if you will, 70 years ago, hasn't been broken since. I'm comforted by this language. I suspect that, if a future occasion of this nature arises, number one, there's no statutory basis for providing an automatic exemption; we will have a hearing like this. It will be decided upon the facts of the case, just as you both have suggested today.

Mr. Cohen, would you agree with that analysis?

Dr. COHEN. Yes. But, I would add to that that I—it seems to me it's very important that the committee and the members of it make very clear the principles that they—that are guiding them, and how they think about the law, going forward, so that there's a record. You know, in the same way that I think both of us looked at the record of the testimony in the Marshall case, that people will go back and look at the record, and, most importantly, look at the things that you Senators said at the time, to help them think this through.

If I could, just—you know, I figured I had taken a swipe at the Obama administration, I've taken a swipe at the Trump administration. Taking on Congress, too, just seemed to be a little bit too much, even for me.

[Laughter.]

Senator KING. The other subject that's come up today which I think is important is the danger of a development of a military case cast. I was discussing this recently with a high-ranking officer in charge of personnel who indicated that something over 80 percent of the current servicemembers come from military bloodlines or from military families. I think that is—and he said, "That's a dangerous situation, because we don't want our military separated from the society." When we made a decision about all-volunteer service, that created a professional military. I completely concur with the idea of broadening ROTC and broadening recruitment efforts so that we don't have a separate group that feels separated from the rest of the society, particularly the civilian government.

Dr. Hicks, your thoughts?

Dr. HICKS. I completely agree with that. I'm from a military family, myself. It is a way of life, and it can seem, I think, for those who haven't lived it, extraordinarily odd and nomadic in nature. I think it's dangerous when we start to look at folks from military families as sort of a self-perpetuating cone of future military service, and the rest of society going about its business differently. So, I do think that's a danger.

Senator KING. It also makes it too easy for the rest of society—meaning Presidents and Congresses—to talk about wars and deployment of troops if there's no widespread of—element of sacrifice.

Dr. COHEN. If I could, I think that's true, but I would also just caution that, as you go forward with this, the military personnel bureaucracies will not be on your side. You know, the easiest, the most efficient thing, from their point of view, is—go to those parts of the country or to those universities which have massive ROTC programs that they can bring in, obviously, from—they—I mean, I've had these kinds of discussions with people—they—if you look at, say, efforts to try to get ROTC back on the Harvard campus, the opposition was not from President Larry Sommers. The opposition was actually from the United States Army. I hate to say that, having been a former—having been an Army officer at one time. But, it was—they just thought it was too much of a pain in the neck, "We'd have to deal with the Harvard faculty, wouldn't be that high a yield of officers, blah, blah, blah," and completely missing this larger point of the connection—having a connection between people who wear the uniform and people who are going to end up in positions of leadership in other sectors of our society.

Senator KING. Thank you.

Thank you both for your excellent testimony.

Thank you, Mr. Chairman.

Chairman MCCAIN. Senator Sullivan.

Senator SULLIVAN. Thank you, Mr. Chairman.

I appreciate the outstanding testimony. Professor Cohen, I want to thank you for your service to our Nation. As usual, your testimony is very insightful and helpful.

You know, just as someone who served as a Marine Corps staff officer to the CENTCOM [United States Central Command] Commander and then later as an Assistant Secretary of State, I can—I certainly agree with your sense of the imbalance between DOD resources and the State Department, which I think we need to look at. But also, I think it's helpful in this discussion on ROTC. I certainly hope that all universities will heed the call to establish ROTC programs.

You know, Senator Warren was talking about this issue. Where she taught and where I went to college, you just name the university, where I—when I went to Harvard, the Spartacist Youth League, which was a organization for young Communists, was allowed to meet on campus, but if you wanted to be part of the ROTC, you were not welcome. I think that was an embarrassment. It took 40 years to get ROTC back after it was kicked off the campus there. The opposition was the professors and the faculty, who were extremely anti-military. I think we should be looking at all universities that continue to ban ROTC, and penalize them. So, hopefully, we'll continue to focus on this.

You know, there's a lot of talk about 1950. You're both historians. Let me just ask the basic question. In a historical context, is that waiver now viewed as something that was in the U.S. interest? Is it—do most historians agree on that?

Dr. COHEN. I think people understand why Truman did it. I mean, Johnson was really a very dysfunctional Secretary of Defense. Everybody hated him. He was clearly not the right guy to supervise a substantial buildup. There was a bit of a whiff of desperation about this. I think the general consensus is that, although Marshall did some good things as Secretary of Defense, you know, he was not—does not go down as one of the best Secretaries of Defense, by a long shot.

Senator SULLIVAN. But, the historical record's not widely critical of it, is it?

Dr. COHEN. No.

Senator SULLIVAN. Are the analogies that many of my colleagues have raised today about, you know, Senate—or Dr. Kissinger testifying before the committee last year about the world—the United States not facing—you know, hadn't seen this many crises since the end of the World War II. Some of us are concerned about a hollowed-out Army. Are those—and the character and reputation of General Mattis—are those historical analogies apt when you look at 1950 and General Marshall?

Dr. COHEN. I think they go a little bit too far. I mean, the United States military was in much worse shape in 1950. You know, if you know the history of the Korean War, it is a pretty sorry tale, with a few exceptions in that first year, as we were putting ourselves back together. I think the overall sense of threat was much greater, because, you know, again, there really was this chance that you'd have World War III. So, it's not——

Senator SULLIVAN. Can I ask you—and let me just—sorry to cut you off, but—let me ask about kind of a question that relates to the Korean War. You know, there's a conventional wisdom—and we've heard it today, we've heard it in the media a lot on this issue—that there's a growing trend of military influence in our government. But, is that really the case? Let me give you a couple of counter-examples.

With the incoming Trump administration we'll have now, three out of the last four Presidents will have not served in the military. Much of the Obama White House staff never served in the military. Congress now has 20 percent veterans. In 1971, it was 73 percent veterans. In your view, can this create situations where important military matters are not well understood or emphasized by civilian leaders?

Let me give you one that relates to the Korean War. That's the issue of rigorous military training. Very, very difficult, hard, dangerous military training. I think sometimes people aren't comfortable with that. I think sometimes Members of Congress don't understand it. When you don't have military training, you end up with, you know, situations like Task Force Smith in the Korean War. General Mattis certainly understands that. I've talked to him about it. But, do we risk, when we don't have much military experience in our civilian government, that other leaders don't understand what Task Force Smith is? I guarantee you a lot of the members of the Obama White House right now don't even know what I'm talking about. Isn't that an issue that we should be concerned about, as well, rigorous military training and having people who actually understand those kind of military issues through their own military service, which is increasingly less and less in our civilian government?

Dr. HICKS. Senator Sullivan, I—first of all, I think military readiness and training is a major issue. I do know what Task Force Smith is. But, I do not believe you have to have served in the military in order to have knowledge and appreciation of the profession of arms. Is it different than serving? Absolutely.

Senator SULLIVAN. I'm not talking knowledge and appreciate, I'm talking about rigorous military training.

Dr. HICKS. Understand. Again, I do think—as I said before, I do think there's a distortion when you have a society that's becoming less familiar with the military, that has had less service in the military. I think it's a problem when there is distrust between the military and civilian leadership. I think we can point to instances both in the current administration and in the Bush administration and throughout history where that has—those tensions have moved from helpful to unhelpful. But, I—the only thing I'm going to say—and obviously, it's biased, because I have not served in the military, but I have dedicated my entire professional life to the Department of Defense and service—that I do not think you have to have served in the military in order to be an effective civilian leader in military affairs.

Dr. COHEN. I completely agree with Dr. Hicks on that. I don't think prior military experience makes any difference to those kinds of things. You know, they're—again, we can have a long discussion about the history of training in the United States military. They had to completely overhaul our training in the middle of World War II, which was completely in the hands of the United States Army. It was partly because they had had no combat experience, and they found themselves having to change things.

Our greatest Commander in Chief was a man with zero military—or almost zero military experience: Abraham Lincoln. The other competing Commander in Chief, Jefferson Davis—distinguished war record, chairman of this committee's predecessor—he was a terrible Commander in Chief, luckily. So, I don't think that, per se, military experience is what matters, although I think it's a good thing.

The fact is, we're not going to get it back. You know, in 1971, the World War II vets were still around, and dominated Congress. Well, that's not coming back. I think we have to accept that and find other ways of doing with it.

But, I very much agree with Dr. Hicks, it's important not to denigrate people who have not served, for whatever reason.

Chairman MCCAIN. Could I say, Dr.—both doctors—I totally agree. Some of the challenges we face in the military today, particularly the much needed reforms in acquisition and other areas, require talents that have nothing to do with the military. I agree with you, some of our finest leaders have not—it should not be a requirement.

Thank you.

Senator Shaheen.

Senator SHAHEEN. Thank you, Mr. Chairman.

Thank you, to both of our panelists, for your testimony and for your thoughtful and pragmatic approach to this issue. Because I think this is an issue that it may not be helpful to be doctrinaire on.

You know, I totally agree with the statements that have been made that it's important for the country to have skin in the game when it comes to military engagement and conflict around the world. As a—someone who came of age during the Vietnam era, I very clearly remember the debate over draft versus a volunteer—All-Volunteer Army. I think some of the ideas about what would happen at the time have not proved to be accurate, and we have a very professional, very well-trained military. But, it's only about one percent of the population who actually have skin in the game, and that that's not healthy for the long-term future of the country.

Now, having said that, I want to pick up on the comments you just made, Dr. Cohen, because, in 2002, for the Washington Post, you wrote an article called "Hunting Chicken Hawks," where you made the point that I think you've just made, which is that there's no evidence that generals, as a class, make wiser national security policymakers than civilians. So, I wonder if you can talk a little bit more about that, beyond just Lincoln and Jefferson Davis, and what you've seen that makes you come to that conclusion.

Dr. COHEN. Well, it's a result of, basically, being a military historian. I—you know, if you look at things like the Vietnam War, where there have been some very interesting books, including one by my friend H.R. McMaster, "Dereliction of Duty," all about the Joint Chiefs not standing up to Robert McNamara, my reservation about the book—and I've talked to General McMaster about this—is, it's not like they really had a better idea. I mean, when you really press into the history of the Vietnam War, did they have a different conception which would have allowed us to achieve our national objectives?

You know, this is why in my book, "Supreme Command," I talk about an unequal dialogue. It has to be a dialogue. It has to be give-and-take. At the end of the day, the civilians are responsible, the civilians are accountable. The military absolutely has to be heard, and they have a duty to speak up. But, it—it can only be forged in a dialogue. I think the—we have to be very careful in our understanding of, What is the nature of military expertise? Because when you go to war, you're trying to use force to achieve political purposes. I—if I might, I'd say one other thing, which is, I do think it's important to have skin in the game. Speaking as someone who had skin in the game, you know, I was in favor of the Iraq War, and my son went off and fought in it twice. I would have been in favor of it in exactly the same way, I think, if he hadn't made that decision entirely on his own, actually before 9/11, to join the service. It does affect how you think about things. It affects how you think about the political leadership. It affects about how you hold them accountable. But, I think, if you're a serious individual, I don't think it actually changes how carefully you weigh decisions about sending young men or young women into harm's way.

Senator SHAHEEN. So, I think the argument that I find most persuasive, that you make, Dr. Cohen, and, to some extent, you also made it, Dr. Hicks, about why this waiver at this time might be appropriate, is because of your comments that a Secretary Mattis might be a stabilizing and moderating force preventing stupid, dangerous, or illegal things from happening in the incoming administration. So, with that in mind, I want to ask you a little bit more about an issue that Senator Perdue raised with respect to the interaction between the National Security Council, under former General Flynn, and the Department of Defense and how policy might get made with that kind of interaction.

So, do you have any insights, either one of you, into what we might expect and who we might expect to come out on top in those kinds of debates about what policy should be?

Dr. HICKS. Senator, I would be foolish to predict what is going to happen here. I think, in any administration, you see, in the first 9-plus months, for really the cycle of Congress, some shaking around, if you will, inevitably in every administration; and there is a particularly combustive combination, potentially, in this set of factors we have coming in, in a few weeks. So, I can't predict what that will look like.

I do want to add to the very good comments that Professor Cohen made earlier with regard to this issue of the National Security Council's role and the President's ability to choose his own staff, that it's always important for the Secretary of Defense, of course, but also throughout the national security system, to remember that the National Security Advisor is not in the chain of command. That sounds so very straightforward, but, in the day-to-day actions inside an administration, it can become confusing about whether that National Security Advisor, to use Professor Cohen's words, is a principal or not.

Certainly with regard to where orders come from, how they are communicated—is it from the President, is it from the National Security Advisor?—I think that tension, which, again, is present in many administrations, will play itself out here, and we will see what the answer to your question is very soon.

Dr. COHEN. Once again, I agree with Dr. Hicks. You know, you—it seems—I also have no idea what this will turn into, but, from what I've read of the President-elect's decisionmaking style, he likes to have lots of competing power centers competing for his ear, and jockeying around and bouncing into each other. My personal preference is for orderly processes, but, then again, I'm not President, so I don't get to make that decision. I think there will be a lot of pushing and shoving.

Senator SHAHEEN. Thank you both.

Chairman MCCAIN. Senator Nelson.

Senator NELSON. Flynn versus Mattis and Kelly. That's going to be an interesting tension. A three-star versus two four-stars. But, the three-star has the President's ear daily. You want to comment on that?

Dr. COHEN. I think you summarized it very well. It is one of the arguments, in the long run, for not having retired general officers in these—you know, in a position like Secretary of Defense or even possibly as National Security Advisor, because they never forget their rank. I have yet to meet a General who says, "Please, just call me Bob." Well, that's not entirely true, but their—you know, their rank carries with them after they retire. That's just a psychological fact that you cannot get around.

Senator NELSON. Dr. Hicks, you used the term "self-perpetuating cone of military service." That's going to occur as long as we don't have a draft, isn't it?

Dr. HICKS. Well, I don't necessarily think that's true. I certainly don't recommend a return to a draft. I do think, inevitably—we don't need a military, let's say, two to three times the size it is now. I think most people would agree with that. So, we're not really looking to vastly grow the size of our military; and thus, the percent of the population. It really gets back to the issue of, Is it all occurring—is all that recruitment and accession occurring within a population that's never changing? That's not healthy, if that's true.

It goes back to some of the issues about looking for new pools of interest. That obviously can relate to opening up, for instance, positions to women, looking at areas like cyber, new skillset areas, where different types of people, maybe, would be attracted to service than have been before and that we need.

So, I think there are a variety of ways to get at this issue. I don't think there's a single solution. It's certainly not the draft.

Dr. COHEN. Dr. Hicks said it better than I could.

Senator NELSON. Dr. Cohen, you gave the dramatic example of civilian control of Truman over MacArthur. Can you think, in history of the country, any examples in reverse, where the military has actually overcome the civilian control? Maybe other countries. But, you——

Dr. COHEN. Oh, I mean—yeah, but that—well——

Senator NELSON. Not a dictatorship, a democracy. You mentioned the situation in Israel.

Dr. COHEN. Well, you know, the most effective Israeli Minister of Defense was also the Prime Minister, David Ben Gurion, who leveled out as a junior corporal in the British Army, I think, over a period of about three months in World War I. I think anybody who knows anything about Israeli military history knows he was far and away the most effective Minister of Defense that they ever had. He's really the guy who built the Israel defense forces.

Whereas, conversely, let's say, if you look at the Yom Kippur War, Moshe Dayan, great military hero, in many ways got in the way. It was Prime Minister Golda Meir who ended up being a much more effective strategic decisionmaker, working with the chief of staff. So, I'd say Dayan in the 1973 war is a pretty good example of that.

By and large in the United States, you know, the civilians always win. Not—but not without, occasionally, some serious pushing and shoving.

Chairman MCCAIN. "An American Caesar."

Senator NELSON. Yes.

Dr. HICKS. May I just simply add—I want to answer that question a different way than I'm sure you intended it, but—it bears stating here that there are heavy political costs sometimes for exercising that civilian control of the military. The MacArthur case is a good example. MacArthur was very popular. Truman was very much not popular. He returned, after being fired, to tickertape parades. Truman didn't seek an additional term in office. In fact, the next general was Eisenhower, who had been an aide to MacArthur. So—and I think you could even look at the McChrystal issue more recently and the sort of—the—where the political or the public weight of approval of the military may be very strong, and, even when civil-military analysts look at it and say, "Yes, these are good cases of exercising civilian control," there can be a significant political cost to pay for that.

Senator NELSON. What was the cost that the President paid in firing [General Stanley] McChrystal?

Dr. HICKS. Well, I think that will be left to historians, but my view is that there is a lack of trust between the military and the Obama senior leadership, as Senator Sullivan said, and particularly in the White House. I think, you know, to the extent that that might have further fueled that sense of distance, I think that's a possibility. But, I haven't seen any actual historical reporting on that.

Chairman MCCAIN. Senator Blumenthal has arrived.

Senator BLUMENTHAL. I wish that were true. Thank you, Mr. Chairman.

[Laughter.]

Senator BLUMENTHAL. Thank you, Mr. Chairman.

I want to thank the Chairman and the Ranking Member for holding this hearing, because civilian control over the Department of Defense and the military in general is really a bedrock principle, one of the founding principles of this democracy recognized from the inception of our great Nation. I have deep respect for General Mattis and his service to this country, having met with him over numerous years and having had the benefit of his advice and insights over my service in the United States Senate.

We're here today to discuss, in general, the issue of civilian control over the military and how that principle is served, or not, by his appointment. But, the general issue applies, regardless of what we think of him. To emphasize the uniqueness of the waiver contained in this statute, Congress included a nonbinding section expressing the intent that Marshall's waiver was to be an exception, quote, "This Act is not to be construed as approval by the Congress of continuing appointments of military men to the office of Secretary of Defense in the future," and—end of quote—and, quote, "No additional appointments of military men to that office shall be approved," end quote.

I'm concerned—I think many of us are—that a waiver here would set a precedent. I wonder if you have advice to us as to how a waiver here can avoid setting precedent. I know, in response to one of the questions previously, I think perhaps by my colleague Senator Reed, you have emphasized a waiting period or a period of time as avoiding the repetition of that precedent, but the exception may swallow the rule. My question to you is whether there is anything by way of legislative intent in what we may have to say about doing a waiver here, or perhaps even in the legislative statutory language, whether we can assure that, in fact, we are making a very unusual and unique exception so as to avoid some of the concerns, the general concerns that have been expressed, even if we want to move ahead with General Mattis's nomination and confirmation.

Dr. COHEN. Senator, I'm no expert on draftsmanship of the law, but I—you know, I do think it makes sense to put things into the text of the law that make it very clear just how exceptional you all believe this case is.

The one other thing which I suggested in my testimony, which may or may not be helpful, is that you consider restoring the ten year rule and going back from the seven year rule. I think that would be, actually—that would send a certain message about how seriously Congress takes that. But, that would be my only additional thought. I'm not—I'm—and that really, obviously, is a matter for you folks to deliberate on.

Dr. HICKS. I would just add, I think, again, that the very narrow way in which the legislation, as I have it in front of me at least, is construed is very helpful, and, as you point out, the additional language with regard to how exceptional—and, you know, I think in generational term—people may want to use different language, but—generationally exceptional this decision would be.

Senator BLUMENTHAL. I would just point out, it's an obvious point, that—the difference between 10 years, 7 years, 3 years, 15 years—these are all sort of arbitrary time periods. I don't know of the fact-based justification for any specific numbers of years. It's more the principle that's important. So, I do agree that the language is narrow, but I'm just trying to, in effect, narrow the intent so that it's clear to future Presidents—or this President, for matter—that it is truly an exception based on General Mattis's extraordinary qualifications and the very extraordinary time in which we live.

Thank you.

Thanks, Mr. Chairman.

Chairman MCCAIN. I think Senator Gillibrand has asked for another question.

Senator GILLIBRAND. No. Thank you, Mr. Chairman.

Senator REED. Oh.

Chairman MCCAIN. No?

I thank the witnesses.

I don't know why, Dr. Cohen, I was reminded of—probably one of the seminal moments was the firing of Harry Truman, an authentication of civilian—the adherence of civilian control of the military, since he was the most popular man at the time. Truman, in later years, said, "I didn't fire MacArthur because he was an SOB, which he was." He said, "I fired him because he was dumb." Do you remember that quote? As only Harry Truman could have put it. An individual that history treats with much more admiration and respect than it did at the time. The more I study, the more I appreciate that seminal moment. It took enormous courage to dispense with the services of, arguably, one of the most popular Americans. It's hard to describe the way Americans revered war heroes at that time.

Would you have any closing comments? Or have you had enough?

[Laughter.]

Chairman MCCAIN. I thank the witnesses. This has been very helpful.

[Whereupon, at 11:32 a.m., the hearing was adjourned.]

○